Legal Off

Tax Havens

How to Take Legal Advantage of the IRS and Pay Less in Taxes

By Jesse A. Schmitt

LEGAL OFFSHORE TAX HAVENS: HOW TO TAKE LEGAL ADVANTAGE OF THE IRS CODE AND PAY LESS IN TAXES

ISBN-13: 978-1-60138-257-3   ISBN-10: 1-60138-257-X

Library of Congress Cataloging-in-Publication Data

Schmitt, Jesse A. (Jesse Albert), 1979-
  Legal offshore tax havens : how to take legal advantage of the IRS Code and pay less in taxes / by Jesse A. Schmitt.
      p. cm.
  Includes bibliographical references and index.
  ISBN-13: 978-1-60138-257-3 (alk. paper)
  ISBN-10: 1-60138-257-X (alk. paper)
  1. Tax planning--United States--Popular works. 2. Income tax--United States--Foreign income--Popular works. 3. Investments, Foreign--Taxation--Law and legislation--United States--Popular works. 4. Tax havens--Popular works. I. Title.

  KF6297.S29 2008
  343.7305'23--dc22
                          2008014104

INTERIOR LAYOUT DESIGN: Vickie Taylor • vtaylor@atlantic-pub.com

Printed in the United States

Printed on Recycled Paper

Dedication

To my best friend and wife Katie, who never stopped loving me, to my friends in the theatre who never left my side, and to my new friend Amanda who showed me what is possible. Also to Alan, Muriel, and Peter.

Fractured, yet united; and on we go.

We recently lost our beloved pet "Bear," who was not only our best and dearest friend but also the "Vice President of Sunshine" here at Atlantic Publishing. He did not receive a salary but worked tirelessly 24 hours a day to please his parents. Bear was a rescue dog that turned around and showered myself, my wife Sherri, his grandparents Jean, Bob, and Nancy and every person and animal he met (maybe not rabbits) with friendship and love. He made a lot of people smile every day.

We wanted you to know that a portion of the profits of this book will be donated to The Humane Society of the United States.

–Douglas & Sherri Brown

THE HUMANE SOCIETY
OF THE UNITED STATES©

The human-animal bond is as old as human history. We cherish our animal companions for their unconditional affection and acceptance. We feel a thrill when we glimpse wild creatures in their natural habitat or in our own backyard.

Unfortunately, the human-animal bond has at times been weakened. Humans have exploited some animal species to the point of extinction.

The Humane Society of the United States makes a difference in the lives of animals here at home and worldwide. The HSUS is dedicated to creating a world where our relationship with animals is guided by compassion. We seek a truly humane society in which animals are respected for their intrinsic value, and where the human-animal bond is strong.

Want to help animals? We have plenty of suggestions. Adopt a pet from a local shelter, join The Humane Society and be a part of our work to help companion animals and wildlife. You will be funding our educational, legislative, investigative, and outreach projects in the U.S. and across the globe.

Or perhaps you'd like to make a memorial donation in honor of a pet, friend, or relative? You can through our Kindred Spirits program. And if you'd like to contribute in a more structured way, our Planned Giving Office has suggestions about estate planning, annuities, and even gifts of stock that avoid capital gains taxes.

Maybe you have land that you would like to preserve as a lasting habitat for wildlife. Our Wildlife Land Trust can help you. Perhaps the land you want to share is a backyard — that's enough. Our Urban Wildlife Sanctuary Program will show you how to create a habitat for your wild neighbors.

So you see, it's easy to help animals. And The HSUS is here to help.

The Humane Society of the United States
2100 L Street NW
Washington, DC 20037
202-452-1100
www.hsus.org

Table of Contents

Prologue

What is an offshore tax haven? Is there such thing as a legal offshore tax haven? Is that something which only works for the rich and well-to-do? How can I make the legal offshore tax haven work for me?

These are questions which will be addressed in this book. Along with this we will try to make sense of all the rigmarole and show how something like this could possibly work for you.

Many people are uncomfortable with their current financial situation yet they have never even dared to ask these questions; moving your money out of your sight offshore is a tenuous prospect and seems both unpatriotic and illegal. Finding yourself planted on a completely different continent without any of the traditional "Western" concepts to which you have become accustomed is another place where many people are not comfortable.

However, if you have always wanted to travel, an offshore

tax haven is one way you can make that dream work. If you have worked your fill and you want to get out of the traps that the American Dream can find itself attached to, making the move to an offshore tax haven might be just your speed. If you have kids who are grown or if your spouse has passed and you need to inject some spunk into your existence, an offshore country which sponsors an offshore tax haven might be the way that you can make that move with comfort and ease.

Offshore tax havens are also a great place to stow away money, set up a trust, or set up a foundation; some countries are a good place to run your business from. If you feel like you need support or guidance or answers about the individual situations, this book will be helpful.

So read on to find out if the offshore tax haven, as it is described in these pages, sounds like something which might be of interest to you. This book is meant to be a guide; it is step one in the long trajectory of your experience in enjoying the benefits and risks associated with the legal offshore tax haven. You should always make sure you seek the advice of a lawyer, tax attorney, or someone else who specializes in this type of arrangement before you make any moves. This will ensure that all the proper steps have been taken and that details have been checked off before you set off on your globetrotting adventure.

Introduction

People have probably heard of offshore tax havens, but many do not believe such places exist. Or, they believe they exist, but do not think they are applicable in their situation. Some might not believe in the overall benefit, all things considered. Many people are skeptical and have more questions: What is a legal offshore tax haven? When can I make one work for me? How can I utilize an offshore tax base for my life right now? Do I need to relocate in order to take advantage of this benefit? Where can I learn more?

These are legitimate questions to ask and are questions that we will try to answer in this book. There are applications for an individual or small business in shielding their assets from taxation; you do not need to be a millionaire to take advantage of services such as offshore tax havens. Everyone's money is relative; that is, even for the person with a comparatively small amount of money to a billionaire. His or her tens of thousands of dollars per year are valuable; so why should this person not be allowed to take advantage of the offshore tax havens which apply to his or her situation?

Taxes seem a destined part of our engagement in a society; anyone who has ever gotten a paycheck is able to understand the sting of taxes in our daily lives. Nearly one third of the income from our jobs goes to taxes. In the average lifetime of an average worker, he or she can expect to pay literally hundreds of thousands of dollars in taxes. There are and have been growing movements of people who are fed up and do not want to take it anymore. The growing consensus is that people are happy being self-reliant and are tired of haranguing social programs, and the dependency that their bloated government places on the hard-working, successful individual in lieu of the much lazier and needier recipient.

It could easily be argued that there are times when the taxation on an individual or business is excessive. There are never enough of many things, and time and money always seem to be slipping through our hands. There is a finite tolerance we all have with things like being overtaxed and underrepresented. For those with the ability and constitution to do so, the legal offshore tax havens offer an alternative to the life we all were brought up being told we had to live. Baseball, hot dogs, apple pie, and a 1040 form is not the life that we all dream of; in fact, there are many of us who would argue that the "American Dream" is not even for everyone. With that in mind, it is important to remember that there are reasons to consider the offshore tax haven.

There are many intricacies to the tax code which make it a wise idea to consult with someone before making such a drastic move as manipulating all your worldly assets to a foreign nation. However, taking such steps can increase your net worth exponentially, allow you to put more into your business, and allow you to live the kind of life which you deserve.

While I am no expert by any stretch of the imagination, these are the words of experts who are learned about these different forms of tax savings. There is an entire subculture where people are gravitating toward a like-minded place; if you are of this same persuasion, then you should read on. Even if you are unsure but would like to have a reference guide, this book should serve you well.

While there are many different solutions to reach this same end, they come with different levels of involvement and different levels of upheaval in your own personal life. If you are comfortable living where you are right now, and just would like to have some money stashed away so you can have savings, or have something to pass along to your next-of-kin, then there is an answer for you. If you are fed up with the American system, if you want to get out as soon as possible, or if you want to move away to a faraway country, there is an answer for you. In short, there is a way for everybody to be happy. For those who do not want to pay as many taxes, there is a way to get some relief.

If you are reading these words and feel like you have stepped into an alternate reality that you thought did not exist outside your own mind, you are not alone. The thought that this was real when I began writing this book did not even cross my mind. I thought it must be something for the extremely wealthy, privileged, or for certain people for whom special rules apply and who do not even need the savings in the first place. I came to discover that legal offshore tax havens are real and that the legal offshore tax havens are available even for the average worker who does not have a lot. Just getting started is perhaps the most daunting part of establishing an offshore tax haven; some would view any move as an expensive one to make. This thought is further exacerbated if you are weighing moving all of your assets offshore permanently. In short, it is not something which should be entered into lightly. However, if you are considering putting up some capital, and dipping your toe in, so to speak, you may find what many do; that the savings will be worth it to you; even if you do not have a substantial amount of money to put into it in the first place. There are different answers for everybody and they all can be different and they all can be right for your particular situation. This book will help you to find the answers which are right for you.

What Are Offshore Tax Havens?

Get Up & Go

While many people have many different preconceptions about offshore tax havens, the truth is at once much more complicated than anybody could imagine, yet strangely simple. Once you become familiar with the language of the enterprise as well as the concepts of engaging in an offshore tax haven, it illuminates itself nicely. The facts are fairly apparent that most people, when they discover all the elements of an offshore tax haven, shy away from it or lose interest. As with anything, you should seek counsel on this matter before going through with anything proposed, and you should be comfortable and have a full understanding of all the components. Before addressing all the good stuff that people reading this book are interested in — tax freedom — we need to be able to define exactly what an offshore tax haven is.

Domestic Workers Temporarily Relocated

This is one of the more common types of people this book is reaching out to. Many people who are relocated to a different country, for work or by choice, still hang on to skewed beliefs about their tax status. They could exist for years away from America and think they are free and clear; the fact remains that if the event ever arises that these workers are audited, they could have quite a few worries. For this reason knowing the rules will always work in your favor.

Some people living out of the country believe that none of the income they earn abroad is taxable. That is not correct. Others believe that all of their income which they earn when they are out of the country is taxable. That is not correct either. The truth is somewhere in between, and it all goes back to something known as the "foreign earned income exclusion," which has earned the nickname of the "$70,000 offshore loophole." This is a provision in the American tax code which states that U.S. citizens who live and work outside of the United States may exclude their foreign earned gross income up to $70,000 from taxation.

This is one of the same "loopholes" which many politicians are talking about wanting to close in their presidential campaigns. While it may seem like it is a good bit of stumping rhetoric during the campaign season, closing off an exclusion like this does not do anyone any good. The people who are taking advantage of this are often left having to supplement this "extra" income in costs incurred in a foreign country or the weakening strength of the U.S. dollar against something like the European Euro. No politician has ever won either by trying to give the short end of the stick to his or her constituency.

This domestic-worker temporarily relocated stipulation also comes with a few other added provisions. There is also an employer-provided housing allowance which is excluded from income. If you are a married couple, then your income threshold goes up to $140,000 in addition to the housing allowance. While this has maintained the nickname "$70,000 loophole," there have been increases in recent years in the income threshold; you must see what the exact number is at the time you are planning to leave the country.

There are a few requirements to get these benefits: You must establish a tax home in a foreign country, you must pass a foreign-residence test or physical presence test, and you must have earned income. These are three commonly misconstrued elements as well, and should be investigated more fully.

Where Is My Home?

If you are an American citizen who is fortunate enough to be such a world traveler that you do not have much of a home, you need to know what the IRS thinks about that. If you ask the Internal Revenue Service where your home is, they will tell you it is the location of your principal place of business; as far as they are concerned, you are taxed where you work, not where you live.

But they know what they are doing. The bottom line is that the government does not want to lose any of their leaves, so once they have given you a spot on the branch; it is hard to shake free. The federal government added a caveat which says that, to qualify for the foreign earned income exclusion, you not only need to work overseas, but you also have to establish a place of residence there. So, keeping a home, an apartment, or address in the United States can still cost you 30 to 40 percent of your income with some small exceptions. To fully qualify for this foreign earned income exclusion, you need to sell or rent your property and establish a residence outside of the United States.

How Many Days Are Enough?

You know you need to be gone but you are not sure how to calculate the days. You know you can only be somewhere so long or else you need to be a nonresident or apply for some kind of paperwork. Being a human being on this earth, at this moment, is a complicated endeavor. However, there are great rewards to be had and there are ways that you can turn the system around in your favor and set to the task of having the bureaucracy work for you. But before we get to all that, we need to establish where you are and for how long.

Physically Present

The second part of this foreign earned income tax exclusion is the physical presence test. This is a fairly cut-and-dried assessment of what your home is and this tends to be the trend for most nations of the world. To qualify for the IRS distinction of being abroad you must be outside of the United States at least 330 days of the previous 12 months. While the days do not need to be consecutive, you need to be careful about your calculations, because people's assignments typically do not begin on January and do not end on December 31. Typically, people are not able to claim the full $70,000 tax exclusion until their second year away from the country. For this reason, it may be worth it for you to speak with a tax professional for reasons of prorating income on the $70,000 tax exclusion for the first tax year you were away.

Also, you can only count whole days spent outside of the United States. There are some rules and exceptions when you are talking about days spent traveling or flying over the United States, so long as the origination of the flight was not within the United States. There are a number of particular rules which need to be followed and closely scrutinized before you make any claims. These stipulations should be of particular importance to people who are traveling between the United States and a foreign country, as their day count will become a big deal to them at the end of the year.

Bona Fide

Perhaps an easier way for you to claim a residence in a foreign country is known as the foreign-residence test. If you establish yourself as a legitimate resident in a foreign country or countries and this residence continues uninterrupted for more than a year and you intend to stay there indefinitely, then you will pass this test.

However, you need to be sure to pass this test, because if you do not, then the IRS is going to come after you. You will be considered a transient, and they will require tax revenue. If you look at the tax law, you will see that where you live is a state of mind. If you intend to be somewhere indefinitely and the IRS looks at how attached you are to the country in question, then you could be considered a resident. There are a number of things you should do to establish yourself within the community so that you will be able to be considered:

- **Where you sleep.** One of the first things that the IRS looks for in interpreting your bona fide residence is where you spend your evenings. A resident likely owns a home or has some kind of a lease.

- **Where is your stuff?** If you have a great deal of your personal belongings in the foreign country then that makes it look like you want to stay there for a considerable period of time. However, if you leave your things in someone else's residence, in a temporary storage facility in the United States, or in your vacant property, this makes it appear as though you have intentions of not staying abroad for any period of time.

- **Your former abode.** If you owned a home in the United States, whether that be an apartment or house, and you leave it unoccupied, then that is a clear signal you plan on coming back eventually. For this reason you need to treat your home as a serious part of your decision and you should figure what your intentions are before you do decide to utilize an offshore tax haven. If you vacate, that sends one message; however, if you choose not to sell or rent your home, then it looks like you could be coming back shortly.

- **Papers.** If you are in a foreign country for a period of time, you will need to get around. Two of the first things you should do to indicate your intention of staying is get a foreign driver's license and register to vote. If you maintain your United States driver's license and voter registration, it will not shun you out of the running, but you may want to consider getting a driver's license in your foreign country regardless.

- **Get involved.** If you were a member of many organizations (political, social, and community) when you lived in the United States, then you should show the same level of involvement in a foreign country. It is also a good idea to allow any other memberships in the United States to lapse when you are living in your foreign country. Join similar chapters of similar clubs and organizations in the foreign country when you are there and this will show a viable intent to stay active.

- **Taxes.** When you are talking about the taxes you are going to get charged on a foreign level, you need to understand that foreign countries base taxes on where you live. If you claim you are exempt from foreign tax because you are not a local resident of your host country, then the IRS will step in and consider you a U.S. resident. This is a misconception that people need to be careful about. You do not want to pay more taxes in a foreign country, or not fulfill your obligations in America because of ignorance.

- **Banking.** According to the IRS, this appears to be something of an afterthought and does not seem to qualify or disqualify anyone in particular. However, this could be of importance if you are teetering on the edge of qualification for the foreign-residence test. It should be noted that opening up at least one foreign checking account is probably a good idea even if you maintain your accounts in the United States or elsewhere. Domestic employer direct deposit is a big reason that this does not disqualify people who are living abroad temporarily. It is far easier for an employer to direct deposit into a domestic account than it is for them to do so to a foreign account or mail a paper check.

- **Address.** It is a good idea to always put down your foreign address when you are filling out applications in your attempt to make the move. Particularly on the line where it says "permanent address" — this is something the IRS can scrutinize and, fair or unfair, make a judgment on. If you do not have an address yet when you are filling out any paperwork, do not put down your old address, but rather put down a friend or relative's address who can forward your mail.

While all of this may seem complicated, these are some of the bars you need to pass to qualify as a foreign resident. Many people prefer to wait for their first year abroad to conduct tests so they are more likely assured to reap the benefits of foreign residency.

Put Up

Another complicated step in this process has a great deal to do with you and your actual intentions. Even after you have gone through all these other steps, you need to be able to prove to the IRS beyond a shadow of a doubt that your term in the other country is indefinite. If you have a plane ticket with a return date upon which you will return, then you are not going to be viewed as a foreign resident by the IRS, and you are thus going to have to pay your taxes. Even if your return date is well off in the distance, the government still owns your tax status. In figuring this, the IRS looks at your employment terms. If the terms say you are coming back on a certain date, even if it is a great period of time away, then they will not grant you the tax breaks. If there is any way for you to have your employer spell it out in vague terms — for example, "John will return to his job in the United States at the completion of this job, which will be some point in the future" — then you are much more likely to be granted foreign resident status.

If the terms of your employment contract are for less than one year, after which you plan to return to the United States, then you will have a difficult time establishing your status as a foreigner. However, if the contract of your employment is open-ended or renewable, or likely to lead to a different job, then you will have a much easier time qualifying.

If you have no contract, then the IRS will look at the company's history of foreign employment. This could work in your favor or not. If the company for which you are working has a history of sending people over who come back after three to six months, then you are not likely to get the foreign-resident status; however, if your employer's history is not well defined or if they have sent people over to work at this particular job who are still there, then the facts are well in your favor. You can skew this perception in either manner by showing or withholding whatever information your company has disclosed to you.

For you to attain this status, you need to do your own legwork. If you are truly destined to become IRS void, a great way for you to help your cause is by offering up information which you have gotten to plead your case. For instance, if you have a coworker who has benefited from his or her tax exempt status doing the same or similar work, you should point this out. Another thing you can do is try to make friends in your new foreign home before you have made it over there. If you are able to come into contact with expatriates who have been in a similar situation as yours, this information may be able to help your case. While the IRS is a bureaucracy of seemingly unwieldy proportions, it is run by individuals. Case workers who are assigned to your particular situation may be able to cut through the slog and offer you this status even though the cards may be stacked against you.

Foreign Income

Now that you are working in a foreign country, have established yourself as a foreign resident, and have done all the other necessary steps, you need to determine what of your income will qualify for the offshore qualifier. Remember that your total income cannot be exempted from federal tax; it is only income which is has been foreign-earned.

You need to identify the income you are paid for services rendered in a foreign country. This income may include salary, fees, tips, and any other compensation. Interest, dividends, and capital gains do not qualify. There are also stipulations for the self-employed and you should look into those rules before you claim something for which you are not eligible.

There are plenty of income types which do not qualify for the loophole. U.S. government employees are completely exempt from this loophole. Pension and annuity payments, disallowed moving expense reimbursements, and income received two years or longer after it has been earned are examples of many of the disqualifying stipulations to this exemption.

Closer

While these are loopholes which are available for every person who meets the qualifications, there are ways in which you can disqualify yourself from being able to participate.

Perhaps the biggest mistake many people make is that they do not know the requirements in the first place. If you are an American and you are living in a foreign country, many people assume that they are free from U.S. taxes. These are issues which should always be taken up with a tax attorney or a representative from your company if your work is sending you there. Before you leave, you should understand the terms so you are clear about what you are entitled to. If you are already away, the Web connects us all; take full advantage of it and get connected with a tax attorney who can tell you the rules as they stand and what you can do at that moment.

Even if you qualify for the loophole — you have met all the preconditions and you feel like you have done everything else you need to do — you still need to file a tax return. This is another of the most common ways which people are confused. If you maintain your resident status, then you still need to file. Simply fill out exemption Form 2555, file your tax return, and claim the exemption.

You need to be mindful of this, because there have been recent changes in the tax laws and a great deal more scrutiny is placed on citizens living overseas. Even if you feel that you are out of the country and you are no longer subject to these rules, the IRS can make your life difficult in a number of other ways. If your passport comes up for review or renewal and you have not filed your income tax returns, they can deny your passport application and you can get sent back to the United States. All you need to do is get the Form 2555 and file it.

Other Taxes

The growing movement of people wanting to be free from tax burden is not new; it is not even fully un-American. For the most part, people who are seeking tax refuge are going to many of the traditional tax havens in the world: the Caribbean, Canada, and certain spots in Europe, such as the Netherlands. However, there are other places where people are finding refuge from tax burden; places like Ireland, the United Kingdom, and Central America are gaining a great deal of popularity for the expatriate.

Where you go to find tax refuge depends a great deal upon what type of life you are looking to lead. If you are a fairly insular individual and you are fine with fending for yourself and are comfortable with a medical system which is only as good as the country you are living in, then perhaps the offshore tax lifestyle is for you. However, you must become familiar with the customs and traditions of the foreign nation. You need to understand the people and their ways and be comfortable living with their culture. While much of the world today is technologically advanced, there are a few exceptions.

Global Investing

There are many domestic workers who make a lot of money but are not interested in leaving their comfortable home in the United States. They may have received a large windfall from an inheritance, have worked hard for a long time and have a great deal of savings, or are just looking for alternative methods in which to save and invest their money so that it is not taxed. For these people, there are alternatives.

One of the easiest things you can do is invest globally; this adds a level of stability to your life and allows you to reap the benefits of tax-free or low-tax countries in your investments. There may be some initial setup fees, and you may need to incorporate yourself; however, if you have the money and you are fed up with the taxes you are charged in America, many nearby neighbors can be an excellent holding place for your money.

To understand offshore tax haven corporations and trusts, there are a few basic tenets which need to be in place before you are able to take advantage of these benefits. Essentially, your offshore tax haven corporation needs to have two characteristics:

1. These corporations need to be separate from the individual who will guarantee that whatever income is derived from their assets is not considered part of the owner's income.

2. These corporations need to be founded in a host country which has better tax advantages than your home country.

If these essential broad tenets are met, then the investor will be able to control the corporation and their assets without tax debt. This is a classic example of the separation of ownership and control.

There are two essential types of enterprises where this can be advantageous: corporations and trusts. To more fully understand their effect, consumers need to be able to know the difference. Most countries allow corporations; some allow trusts.

Corporations

One of the first considerations you should make when trying to decide whether to incorporate is money. How much money you have can dictate what type of setup is going to be advantageous for you. While many people believe corporations to be big companies, that is not necessarily the case.

Corporations were founded because of debt, and people wanted to separate their business lives from their personal lives and have some stake in their own property regardless of the success or failure of their business ventures. Creating a corporation is like creating a second person; while nobody wants to see their business fail, nobody wants creditors to come after their child's home, their wife's blender, or their husband's lawnmower. Having a corporation sets apart the individual business owner's personal liability from the success or failure of the business. Creditors know that, banks know that, and business owners know that; so they are more willing to do business. A corporation status gives its owner legal autonomy. Another benefit of becoming a corporation is that it allows the business the ability to do business without putting its owners at any personal risk.

To incorporate, two things are needed: the articles of incorporation and bylaws, and the articles of association. When you are setting up your corporation, this is the only spot where cost will come into play in trying to do your legal offshore investing. You would be wise to speak with a lawyer who will draft the articles of incorporation. You also have to have a name for your corporation; your name cannot be the same as a corporation which already exists. You need to have an address for your corporation. Your corporation also will ultimately have to design stated objectives; this may be done as broadly as you wish but cannot be illegal or immoral. Depending upon where your country is, you may be required to state your capitalization; you may also need to have a statement which clearly offers that the company is a limited liability organization.

There may be local laws which you need to adhere to as well, and you should look into them before you make any final decisions. Your lawyer should be able to help you understand the local customs and make sure everything is lined up as it should be. Any information your lawyer asks for should be given, provided that you trust the lawyer.

Once you have decided on your articles of incorporation, you should get right to the task of your articles of association. These are typically submitted to the local governments and give the broad terms of the corporation's aims. These can also vary from country to country, so you should speak to your lawyer as well; but there are a few things that you will probably need to have:

- **Stockholders' meeting.** An annual meeting of owners of stock. Primarily, this is only required for people with a controlling stake in your corporation. At your annual meeting, you need to discuss and approve topics by majority decision, including the business actions of the preceding year and the policy decisions on future actions. You also need to discuss personnel and constitutional issues.

- **Board of directors.** These are the people who make decisions on issues that are too specific for the general stockholders meetings, but which fall outside of the day-to-day management and responsibility of the company.

- **Corporate officers.** This is the cabinet of your corporation; sometimes it is made up of members of the board of directors. You must appoint a president, secretary, and treasurer; these are the individuals who negotiate, represent the company, and make commitments in the company's name.

• **Auditors.** These are the people who do the paperwork. They have to verify the annual accounts, and they are typically not employees or directors of the corporation, but are brought in from an external entity.

While you may think this is out of your league when you are talking about a corporation for your offshore tax haven, you can have local proxies hired by the law firm which is incorporating you in the first place. Once they are appointed, and once you are incorporated, the proxies may be contractually bound to hand over their shares to the majority shareholder, or they may continue to hold the shares on your behalf in the foreign country. The annual meetings do not need to be more than a meeting of one as the majority stockholder sits sipping margaritas on the patio. If local law indicates that a more official meeting must be held, then the savvy business owner will turn it back over to the proxies to conduct these meetings in their stead for small fees.

After all the fees, it may seem like incorporating is not such a great idea. However, if you are incorporating in a country where there is low or no tax on personal income and you take all your personal income from the corporation, then this will reduce your tax burden exponentially.

Where to Trust Your Money

One of the most important things to look for when you are trying to decide where you want to keep your money is the political and social situation of your host country. For example, a country which is under political upheaval and has had regular changes in government is not one of the first places many may wish to consider; however, a country which has a long tradition of stability and relative peace is one which many people aspire toward when they are trying to decipher their tax haven status.

A democratic government with a popularly elected and active government is not one which people typically look toward for tax haven status. However, if there is a two-house legislature which is locally elected and a general assembly and if the political decisions are typically local, then you should be safe from radical changes. You need to look into the history of the country to see trends and their political, economic, ethnic, and social hierarchy so you are not left holding the bag if there is civil unrest.

Where to invest and potentially set up your business operations or live will be addressed in individual fashion from nation to nation. There are many obvious and some not-so-obvious pitfalls which people need to look out for when they are deciding where to invest their money in the world market. You should never rely on hearsay when you are deciding on which country your offshore tax haven should be. If you know people who have had success in one aspect or another of offshore investing, that is fortunate for them. It would be a fool's venture, though, to pick up all or a large portion of your assets, your family, your home, and yourself and move off to an unknown place, of unknown customs, with unknown potential gains and losses without first doing your own homework.

Even if you know people you trust and respect who have had good luck investing in an offshore tax haven, you do not know if the same rules are applicable to you. You do not know if you have the same income threshold qualifiers, you do not know if the rules and laws have changed, and you do not know if there are other variables which would for some reason or another disqualify you or alter the formula in some manner.

Much the same as the idea that no two snowflakes are alike, no two offshore tax have equations are the same either. There are preliminary rules which are put in place, but that is it. So you should approach this as though you are the first one to try this, because in a way, unless you have done this before, you are.

CFC and Considerations to Make

If you are fed up with American taxes, which drain such a substantial portion of your earnings, then you should take things into your own hands. In addition to high taxes, much of these proceeds are, in the eyes of many, wasted. If you are looking to escape from contributing toward the coffer of high taxation, then you have options.

If you are so frustrated that you feel like picking up and leaving the country, then there are some things that you should consider. You should be absolutely sure this is something that you want to do; renouncing your citizenship is a difficult and arduous task and getting your citizenship back is harder still. Also, you do not want to decide in the middle that you have changed your mind. If your mind is made up then, you also should be unencumbered by relationships, children, or elders who may need your support at a moment's notice.

If this situation is yours and you have an elder who may need you to be by their side, or a family, or some other imperative reason that you need to be able to appear in your home country at a moment's notice for an indeterminate period of time, then perhaps moving to and taking advantage of a legal offshore tax haven may not be the wisest idea at this moment. There are the universally accepted rules which generally state that if you are inside of a country for a limited period of time (typically six months, 180, 182, or 183 days) then you are not subjected to the local tariffs of the home country.

However, the dynamics which go into long-term care for an older adult can often necessitate that you be by the side of your elder indefinitely. Even though you may not be earning any money at a job, there is still the mobile job you would have been using for income in the foreign country, dividends from investments, or taxes on inheritance or whatever other stipend that you may have been using for your income which could be subjected to taxes in your country of residence that you were trying to escape.

While the idea of taking an elder parent with you may strike your fancy and may even be amenable to the elder, the truth is that as they age, older people need a stunning array of things. First of all, the extreme variance of things which could go wrong with their health is daunting. Likewise, even the startling array of medicines that an older person is likely to need (and may already be taking) is enough to make any offshore tax haven seeker reconsider out of respect for the parent.

Similarly, while your fancy may be to be out on the seven seas and dashing through many different foreign countries, international waters, or in some other situation, the likelihood that your family would want all these same things is small. While going out on adventures could be alluring to a young child at first flush, the truth of the matter is that children need structure and some kind of order to their lives if they are going to be successful. An offshore tax haven seeker is a life choice for an individual or perhaps a couple; entering a child or children into the equation is most likely a problem just waiting to erupt.

That said, there are options for the domestic entrepreneur who is looking to evade his or her business's tax burden, and one of the best ways to get out of paying taxes in business endeavors is to establish a controlled foreign company (CFC).

A number of countries, including the United States, the United Kingdom, Canada, Australia, Spain, France, and Germany, have CFC tax rules which can end up getting attracted to the tax situation regardless of the fact. There are ways to usurp these rules, and you should be familiar with them before you make any commitment to any one country or another.

One of the biggest considerations people need to make with the CFC is the ownership rules. As last written, the United States' CFC rules defined it as "any foreign corporation of which more than 50 percent of its value or voting stock is owned by United States shareholders on any one day during the taxable year of such foreign corporation." A U.S. shareholder is a United States citizen, or entity such as a company or trust, which is holding or controlling more than 10 percent of the shares. One of the simplest ways to avoid this problem is to establish a trust or foundation which can hold more than 50 percent of the shares.

Also, you can utilize business rules from a tax haven country as long as they have no agreement with the United States in terms of their CFC rules. Another thing you can do is put shares in a trust for the children of owners or in the hands of an offshore relative. A different way you could go with this is to team up with other individuals or companies so that all the shares are sufficiently diversified below the 10 percent requirement. While your personal tax burden would be different in every circumstance, there are clever ways around them all.

While the more beneficial of the different locations of offshore tax shelters tend to be more removed island nations or less developed places in the world, there are tax havens, even for the American citizen, in the United States. There appears to be no rhyme or reason to these facts save this one: The more developed a government is (not necessarily the society; but oftentimes the society as well) then the bigger the tax burden. If there is a direct link to the people from the government and the people are all applying to receive their tax forgiveness at once, then it is likely there will be a sudden awakening of said government and they will impose far greater restrictions and hence more taxes.

How Can This Work for Me?

There are a variety of people who want to make the legal offshore tax haven work for them. After you have decided that you want to partake in this exercise, you need to be able to decide where you and/or your money would like to go to achieve this tax-free status. Then you need to get the ball rolling. You should consult with a professional and make sure that you have dotted all your "i's" and crossed all your "t's," because finding out that you missed out on one small thing and having to pay all the penalties that go along with that can be quite troublesome.

Many people who grew up in an industrial market economy like the United States may be surprised at how many places there are in the world that do not have taxes. Some can be used as hands-off places for people to store personal money, savings, or business assets. However, some people are militant about wanting to move their entire operation to this new tax-free state; many nations require this be the case.

Many countries will allow nonresidents to come and live and conduct their business as long as it is not done domestically. Many places, including Cyprus, Gibraltar, and Bermuda, allow people to live in a tax-free society; but also tie in the reins on the people who want to do this by insisting that new residents do not do business with the locals. There are other types of professionals who can benefit from a situation like this, including artisans, craftspersons, writers, artists, trust-fund babies, and investors. The savvy individuals will be able to make do with whatever they have around them. However, you need to be wary of the discrepancies between different nations so you do not end up stuck in a bad tax situation just because of the source of your money.

Expectations

The expectations game is one of the worst ones to play. Unless you are moving into a private, controlled, gated community and you are bringing your own staff, and everything about the location from top to bottom is selected by you, then you cannot ever know what could be coming your way.

While you may have been the most prepared Boy Scout in your troop, the fact remains that, for most, a new place is uncharted territory. Unless you have some nascent experience in disavowing yourself of your national origins, upending your home life, and selling off all your native possessions, you cannot have any idea what this experience will be like.

You should treat every moment as a new adventure and then you may have some luck in staving off what you think is supposed to happen. So long as you equip yourself with the knowledge that you will have absolutely no idea what is to come and you do not let that bother you, you will be all right.

There will probably be times when you will be uncomfortable and that is normal. Even if you have read every last piece of information about your future home and you already know people who live there, have been there, or have lived and returned, every person's experience is his or her own. What will seem quaint and magical to some may end up seeming uncivil and deplorable to others. If there are key traits to this future home of yours which appear to be questionable, these may be things which go on without the notice of any of the natives. In short, expectations should be left at the door and if you cannot be open and receptive to the experience then you may be better off staying somewhere you know.

Language

In addition, you need to be able to weigh the consideration of whatever language barriers you may be forced to deal with. These issues come with traveling globally and are something that every person should be aware of. Many people in developed and developing countries of the globe speak several of the world's major languages in both business and social settings. But the truth of the matter is, when you are trying to negotiate an amount to be paid to a local grocer, you had better have at least a passing appearance that you understand this person. Because if you are a stranger in a strange land and if you are completely out of your element and are without an entourage, then you could end up paying a great deal more for that melon than you deserve to.

Also of concern with regard to language is the cultural respect. If someone came into your home, business, or town and started throwing his or her arms around, demanding things and babbling incoherently, you would probably call the police. Similarly, you do not want to upset the locals, because if you do not show them respect then you surely will get none in return.

Money

Another problem that many people visiting foreign lands have is their manipulation of the local currency. Just because you are outside of the United States does not mean that whatever country you are in will accept your dollars or operate by the Euro. Going back once more to cultural respect, it is a disadvantage to not know the local currency. Even if you are traveling to multiple spots, stop a flight attendant on the plane and clarify monetary amounts before you get into a fight with an extreme local.

And even though Visa and MasterCard say they are accepted all over the world, that still will not change the fact that wherever you are may not have that advanced system of communication and may not be able to take those cards. Whatever the situation, there is likely a currency exchange at your point of entry into the country and you should take a fistful of Ben Franklins and convert these into the currency of your host country. Do this for your own peace of mind; many of us living in countries like the United States do not know what it is like to be stuck with the wrong currency in hand.

Climate

Many people are also amazed at the huge variances in climate which exist in different parts of the world. If you live in the Northern Hemisphere and you are traveling south of the equator, you have got to reverse your whole understanding of seasons.

The weather will dictate what type of clothes you bring and how many layers you need to wear outside. You should always take more than what you think is necessary; a little bit of warm-weather clothing and a little bit of chilly weather clothes never hurt anyone.

Geography

You should also have a rough idea of the geography. If you are from the plains states in the United States and are going to a country where there is a basin but also 15,000-foot cliff peaks, you should know this. While hopefully many of the people who would be taking advantage of the legal offshore tax haven would know enough to not leave home unprepared, there are always those who think the rules do not apply to them. Just ask the guy leading you up the cliffside by a rope and he will remind you. The rules definitely apply to you.

Religion

The final of these last-minute considerations which you should seriously consider is one of the biggest. Religion is something that intersects with everyone's life in a different and personal way; even more than the most strident supporters from the United States, religion comes into the lives of many in a variety of surprising and radical ways. You need to look no further than the origins of the war between Israel and Palestine or no closer to home than the terrorist attacks of September 11 to realize that people's religion is an important and driving force in their lives.

In a much less dramatic, but still no less important manner, religion affects the people of the world in local ways; this is something that every foreign traveler should be aware of and remember, even when doing something seemingly benign and ordinary. Forgetting your host country's religious practices could be committing a major faux pas. If you are chatting on your cell, texting on your Blackberry, and sending an email right in the middle of a public, religious, outdoor ceremony, this could end up turning the locals against you in a latent yet dangerous way. Besides, you do not want your home nation's rude tendencies badly displayed for the foreign masses.

Final Considerations

There are many things you need to consider when you are considering whether to take refuge in an offshore tax haven. How will this work for me? Where will I live? How long will I be able to continue this? What happens if where I go is not what I had expected it to be? These are all legitimate things to consider. However there are a lot of other things for you to ponder before you make your way out into the unknown. You should, of course, familiarize yourself with your future home. You should probably also visit it before you renounce your citizenship, sell your home, get rid of most of your worldly possessions, and leave all that is familiar to you. It is hard to sever ties you have had for all of your life; it is even more difficult for you to reestablish those ties once they have been lopped off.

For that reason, you should always be mindful of the decisions you make. You need to take all facets into consideration; you should make sure that you file all the proper paperwork, fill out all the correct forms, sign your name on the line, and never act in haste.

Risk

With reward comes implicit risk. As with anything in life, you need to consider all sides of a complex issue. Escaping to a legal offshore tax haven is not something to be entered into lightly. While everything we are discussing in this book is legal and above board, it is not easy. Moving money to an offshore account may appear to be simple; however, even this is not as easy as many would like to believe and there are great risks in doing so.

There are all sorts of legal issues you could get yourself involved in for moving your funds across the borders without proper paperwork. This, in theory, may just be reallocation of assets or shifting things around for your own benefit; however, when things are not done in accordance with the rule of law, you move from being a frugal consumer concerned about his or her long-term well-being to being a money launderer punishable by 5 to 20 years in prison. In an effort to curb the growing discontent with American tax law, there are newer, stiffer rules which dictate things like no possibility for parole. You can lose everything you have, and you may have a half-million-dollar penalty to pay on the other side. So you want to be sure that you have filled out the appropriate paperwork before you engage in something like an offshore tax haven.

On a much larger scale, there are risks that an analytical mind might not even be able to comprehend, like a social uprising. It is difficult to predict social unrest and if your offshore investment winds up in a volatile or otherwise unstable social or civil climate, the results could be disastrous.

By that reasoning, any large amount of people who leave en masse from a particular place — like the United States— may cause panic, prompting those on the verge to take flight. This in turn may elicit rage from those residents who have stood fast to their homes, leading to a social uprising. While such events are unlikely in such an insular and inward-looking place as the United States, it is a point worth considering when you are selecting a host nation for your offshore tax haven.

For our own intents, we are talking about legal offshore investing; while we may be able to illuminate some of the things which are illegal, the primary concern in this book is getting you off on the right foot, asking the right questions, and getting the answers you know you need. However, you should always consult with a tax professional before you decide to make any moves.

There are ways around any potential risk on the domestic front; while you may be entering a volatile social climate or you may not have access to all the same resources you have in the States, there are ways in which you can minimize and effectively eliminate any risk from your decision to parachute into an offshore tax shelter state. Depending on where you go and what you bring with you, what you leave behind and how you get there, you may wind up in an excellent position in your new location.

While there are many naysayers in the world and particularly on the World Wide Web who speak in generalities about the "risks" of offshore investing, these people are the ones mistaking risk for work. There are a lot of hoops to jump through to make the offshore tax haven a full and legal reality in your scope. But if you believe in your position and have courage of your convictions, then there are no two ways around it. When offshore tax havens make sense for you and when you approach them in a legal fashion, the reward is nothing sweeter.

Approach Risk – Spread It Around

Any investor who has been at it long enough will be able to tell you that the best way to avoid risk is to not put all your eggs in one basket. You do not need to be a current events geek to be familiar with a name synonymous with corruption and scandal like Halliburton.

Founded in 1919 in Houston, Texas, Halliburton has become a multinational energy organization over the years. For a company like Halliburton in a business like oil in America, there has been a growing, stinking air of profiteering which has only grown more apparent with the 24-hour-a-day news cycle on television. In addition, having a two-term president in the Oval Office who made his name in Texas oil moves the goalposts even further back. There have been a number of examples of favors for favors done by way of "no-bid contracts" from the United States and the topic "Separate Oil and State" is a major theme of ongoing social texts like "Halliburton Watch" (**www.halliburtonwatch. org**).

Halliburton exposed another chink in the imperial armor of the U.S. government and it was unfortunate for those executives who lost tens of millions of dollars when the bubble burst. But what about the worker? What about the 57-year-old man, ready to retire to his dream life in utopia? He did nothing wrong. He regularly contributed and suffered for it. He paid his dues. He worked the line for 30 years, gave in the maximum, put his belief and all his marbles in this one stinking egg. What about his family? Contributing the max for better than 20 years at better than average returns (as Halliburton was heralded as having) would have left the beneficiary with a hefty payday. Maybe more than one million dollars, which is no small change for anyone; least of all the 9-5'er. Where is their retribution?

What is this honest worker going to do with whatever meager savings he has? It is not even as though this is a particularly remarkable event; in the world of corporate America, businesses are opening and closing their doors all the time. But most do so with some amount of notice to their staff, respect to their workers who brought those at the top such success, and some dignity by living up to their promises by paying out what they owe, at least. Not so for Halliburton, and the worker was the one left holding the bag.

The lesson is to spread your wealth around. You do not want to preclude any one sector because you feel like it is not performing as well as you would like it to; historically, all sectors have given back returns. While you are young, you should be able to take as much risk as you are comfortable with as you have the benefit of time and being able to continue working long after you could potentially lose everything. But through the years you will want to begin moving assets over to a more diversified, conservative position.

While this is not about stock investing, the rules for offshore tax haven investing are no different. Just because you are holed up in one place does not mean your money should be. What happens if your local economy hits a skid or if the country you are living in has social unrest or goes to war?

By that rationale you should not ever live anywhere permanently. You have the benefit of a big world out there! With the rising of the global economy and with formerly closed-off ports opening their doors, there is greater opportunity than ever to make yourself and your life that of the nomadic world traveler.

Do you want to be the one on the front lines, who stands with his or her pitchfork and offspring, trying to fend off the rebel army just because it is the place you call home? Fortunately for you, most of the places that are found in this book have and have had a relatively stable political and social climate for some time. Most of the places which are referenced have a welcoming opportunity for new money and expatriates who are looking to come through and settle down on their shores. The political and social climate is addressed and brought to the fore so people are able to understand what they are stepping into and the risks involved.

Just like any good student, though, this book should not be your sole resource. While this is a thoroughly researched and comprehensively fleeced work, you should do your own independent research if you are seriously considering this course of action. Make sure you speak to a professional and you have filled in all the correct forms so you are comfortable making the decision to leave your home nation and set off on this adventure.

On the other hand, if you decide that the trials and tribulations you have to endure in your own current social climate are worth the costs, and the idea of moving into your own offshore tax haven paradise is just too wild, outlandish, fantastic, risky, or advantageous, then you should do so with a confident mind and a content heart.

Risk Is Relative

What is "risk" to some may not be risky to others. It is important to consider your risk tolerance and how much of it that you are willing to take. If you are an independent person and feel fit and fine, you may be a lot more willing to say "Carpe diem!" and let fate carry you along. But if you are dependent either medically or socially, you may not deal well with the isolation which is part of leaving everything familiar and entering into something unfamiliar, possibly alone.

So if it is a few dollars or if it is your physical and mental health, you may wish to reexamine this question as you read further.

History

George Bernard Shaw said, *"We are made wise not by the recollection of our past, but by the responsibility for our future."* This is particularly pertinent to the offshore tax haven as people fervently try to understand the underlying motivation for doing things. We only have this one life in which to do everything, and our legacy left behind us should be a thing which every person is mindful of. If you murder or steal, then this is the legacy you will leave behind; if you teach or do community outreach, even though the immediate reward may seem small, the impact you have on the lives of those you come across in a positive manner will carry your legacy well beyond your own years.

While offshore tax havens may seem to be tools for the wealthy and aloof, their effect is felt, presently, by only two bodies: the government and the individual. A statement such as that may seem flip, but offshore tax havens have long been the subject of much derision. It goes almost without saying that in American government, something which breaches these two inalienable bodies is not taken kindly.

Offshore tax havens seek separation of the individual from the government and this is seen as something unnatural.

Not like the mother and child whose outgrowth is a real part of life, and whose independence and success are wished and expected, the individual, when born into a society, is more like the recipient of a Mob favor. Despite the fact that a person of a society is cultivated and nurtured and given things, it is always in anticipation of the expected return in both treasure and loyalty. Not surprisingly, then, offshore tax havens have long driven deep into the political divide and despite the widely varying opinions on the matter, it is generally frowned upon by those with an allegiance to the home country.

In an article in *The Economist*, Colin Powell was quoted as saying, *"What...identifies an area as a tax haven is the existence of a composite tax structure established deliberately to take advantage of, and exploit, the worldwide demand for opportunities to engage in tax avoidance."*

As you can see, the government's position against tax havens has always been contentious at best. For a big government, taxes are not only the bread and the butter, but the knife which spreads the butter, the oven which bakes the bread, and the cow which gives the milk which makes the butter. Taxes are everything to a government; without them, the government would cease to exist. So they must consider how to handle dissenters. They posses a sense that this ideology must be squelched lest the movement begin to grow and the government begin to crumble.

And yet all at once the tide of people escaping the grasp of the tax man continues to grow. The overwhelming consensus seems to lead to the same end of the government's ineffective ends. A common belief on the other side is that when something is not working as it should, it should not continue to be funded. This argument seems logical enough at first glance and it is with this argument that many people wish to take advantage of the offshore tax haven. They see their role as a pied piper of sorts, rocking the foundation of society by telling what they see as the truth. And they may have many good points.

Relevance

Some people see no place for the offshore tax haven in civilized society. More likely than not these people are ones who make full use of the government which they were born into; quite likely these people also wish for the greater applications of government into their daily lives. They begrudgingly or willingly pay their taxes and expect a return on this payment by way of quality schools, well-maintained roads, reliable postal service, staffing and maintenance of police and fire services, a good network of local hospitals and clinics, and local officials who represent their larger needs among many other things.

These also are the people who take their two weeks of paid vacation every year, clock in for their 50 weeks at 9 a.m. and out at 5 p.m., expect their retirement to begin the moment they turn 62 and a half, and will squelch anyone who says any differently.

This book is not for those people. Making full use of the offshore tax haven requires a bit more of an adventurous spirit, a moment in your mind when you are able to imagine the possibility of living in a foreign place where you need to learn a foreign language, finding a place in your life where you could imagine spending time out of the country, away from home, maybe for the rest of your life.

There are places which lie in between; places for an American citizen which do not require you to fully leave the United States, where you are able to manipulate the tax laws in your favor. These will be discussed in some depth in Chapter 7.

Overview

Some of the things you need to look for when you are getting involved in using offshore tax havens may be obvious to most people; but not everyone. Some of the potential entanglements are often unheralded, so you should be aware of certain things.

When you are traveling anywhere away from home, you need to be careful for your safety. This is no different than when you are moving your money to a foreign country. If your money is going to be held in an area where there is a great deal of civil unrest, social strife, or major government upheaval of some other kind, you can bet that your money is at high risk. This is something you need to look into before you settle on one country or another, as this is part of the program of being an offshore investor.

You have a whole other set of conditions to be wary of if you are moving to a different area. If you are bringing your family, your home, and all your worldly possessions to a foreign country for an indeterminate period of time, you should be sure you are going to be in a peaceful place or somewhere where you are not going to be victim to any kind of strife.

If you have the ability, you should make a visit to your future host country before you live there permanently. If you have been there in the distant past, you should see if conditions are comparable to when you went there last. You should have an understanding of the language which is spoken in the area; you should not assume that everybody in the world speaks English all the time. If you have any kind of reservations about moving to this new home, then you should speak to a local office which represents the nation. Even if you have to travel a great distance, it could be well worth it for you to find out any things which are not listed in the literature you have read. Speaking to somebody who has lived there is an essential component to understanding how life differs, especially if you are speaking to somebody who now lives in the United States and has for some time. They will have a perspective of what you should do. This will allow you a deeper understanding from what you have read in books or from what other people have told you who have visited the area.

Another thing you need to consider with a conservative eye is the cost. While there are listed prices for everything from movers and moving people to exterminators and repair persons, you should always trend upwards. When you move, there will invariably be unexpected costs incurred, and you need to be able to handle these during the course of the move. This is not a thing that you should take lightly. This is something of permanence, so you should make sure you are handling yourself in the way which is consistent with people who make this move, and if you are having any doubts, you should dispel those before you go. You do not want to get halfway there and decide that; reversing course is difficult indeed.

Before you go somewhere for tax breaks — or move your money somewhere for tax breaks — you also need to consider all of the other potential things which could drain your funds. Some people move out of the United States thinking that everywhere else has less of a tax burden only to discover that they have left the United States to go where the tax situation is much worse. Make sure you speak with a qualified individual who can tell you about the conditions in the foreign country you plan on going to before you get there. Also make sure you research multiple places so you do not put all your stock in what one person or another says. You need to investigate a number of potential places; this is not only all your finances but also your life!

You also need to be clear on the terms of your life and life style. If you are working in this new country, there should be a guarantee that the work is still available and still viable when you get there. If you go somewhere without a worker's contract and without a definite period of time to be living somewhere, you raise the level of risk substantially.

Political Implications

While finances must figure into all of our daily lives and the involvement of government in an individual's day-to-day affairs is often the reason that someone reaches out to something like offshore tax havens in the first place, it is worth examining how relative the facts are in real life.

You may complain with your coworkers about the far-reaching hands of the government and their tax dance, but is this something that is real to you? Are you hurt or helped by the deep pockets of your home nation's government? Is your refund check usually high every year? Do you, your spouse, or your children benefit from the taxes which are spent?

This is a question which deserves close scrutiny and should be considered before you leave your home. Also, do you have an illness which requires regular care? If you were in a grocery store in Detroit and you went into cardiac arrest, there would probably be an ambulance there in minutes and there may even be people on the scene who would be able to help in the interim; however if you were in Siberia and went into insulin shock and you were miles away from the nearest hospital or even another person, would you be able to help yourself in time to save your life?

All these questions and others which are relevant to your life are worth consideration and meditation before you make any final decisions on taking drastic measures like giving up your citizenship so that you can save a few dollars.

Why?

Many people feel compelled to do this dash and squirrel their money from their home country's grasp. There are some who would call this simple greed. However, there is a deeper rift going on in the cultural consensus as the United States has increasingly become the divided municipalities. People are feeling ripped off, unrepresented, and angry; they want a way out. It is these people who should be most interested in the legal offshore tax havens because it is these people who are going to benefit the most from this knowledge. Changing your immediate surroundings may be easy; however, changing your whole way of life is difficult and should not be entered into lightly.

It should not surprise anybody that people are interested in legal offshore tax havens because people want to be free to be able to do the things which make them happy without fear of reprisal. Legal offshore tax havens are mechanisms that can change your life. There is no greater way of changing your life than changing the continent you call home. While many of us feel that this is something that is well out of our league financially, it is not something which is prohibitive to all. There are a number of different types of people who are able to participate in a legal offshore tax haven both in person and in a more passive manner.

It is a natural extension when cultures have begun to intermingle and people have begun to have greater understanding about things outside of what they read in books. The Internet and world travel have pushed the legal offshore tax haven from a concept to a definite reality for many people. They are tired of being told what they are able and unable to do; people want to be in charge of their own lives in more ways than one, so there are many who go this route and they could not be happier for it.

By that rationale, there should be no surprises that the same happens in politics. Both nationally and locally, like-minded individuals gravitate toward one another. If there were ever any doubt about what people who wanted out of the tax system of America believed, then it must be cast aside when they see natural gravitation that people have toward places. The Bahamas, Switzerland, Malta, Panama, and Barbados are just a few of the many places where people go to escape the tax man in America. And now, as these countries become more and more a part of the solution for many Americans, so it goes for the remainder of the world. While there are a few countries that have as much of a bureaucracy and an ineffectual government as the United States, it is true that many people use this guidepost as a marking point in their lives and they all escape to the same countries.

America is not the first to reach this conclusion either. While the original settlers of the 1700s sought to relieve themselves from the strain of the tax burden of England, they only partly achieved that. More to the point, Americans did a standout job of bringing the wrangled mess of their home country to this new land and imposing the exact thing they had hoped to remove from their lives.

To go from one bad situation straight into another is a big risk. For this reason you should investigate all the countries that are available for this situation because you do not want to move somewhere that is inconsistent with your desires just because it is the first legal offshore tax haven you come across. There are numerous places you could go to escape the clutches of the tax man, and they all come with definite advantages and disadvantages. If you are feeling like you need to find out more information, then you should look into many different options before you make any concrete decisions. This is something that will affect the rest of your life, so you should be conservative in your steps and diligent in your thought process.

We all share hopes and dreams for ourselves and for our families. Once you have defined these desires you should make sure that the offshore tax haven you are looking into runs congruent with these ideas. This does not happen with a wave of the hand and no research; the fact is clear that you will need to do a great amount of inspection and investigation so that you are making these choices with a clear head and sound judgement.

If you need to find out more about the different areas to which you are going before you get there, you have resources available to you in your hometown. People who live in and around New York City have the United Nations at their fingertips. While most of us do not live in the five boroughs or Westchester, Suffolk, or Nassau counties, there should be offices in many cities and towns all over the nation. One of the easiest things to do is to search the Internet and see where and what you find in your area.

Newton's Law of motion comes into play when we are talking about legal offshore tax havens, as the natural tendency may be to remain inert. An object at rest tends to stay at rest; but there are a number of reasons for people who are unhappy with their current situation to change it. Even more important, if you are unhappy with your current situation then you *should* change it.

5

Offshore Investment Types

Now that we have defined offshore tax havens and talked about their history, what is next? You need to decide that you are willing to take this step and that you understand what you would be investing in. You also should understand how you plan to invest. For example, do you want to move to your offshore tax haven? Are you interested in making this a hands-off type of investment? Would you like to open up a foreign business? Are you looking toward the future for a retirement home or a "weekend villa"?

All of these are legitimate uses of the offshore investment trajectory and they all come with a varied amount of risk and potential return. For the latter half of this book we will look in depth at many of the most popular offshore tax haven locations and the various types of considerations you need to take. Right now, let us look at the offshore investment types and the potential tax savings you might be able to anticipate.

Offshore Real Estate

One of the biggest investments in offshore tax havens has to do with real estate. While people move tens of thousands or even hundreds of thousands of dollars to offshore accounts or other types of corporations, most often, when people make a move to another country, they buy land or a home. Buying offshore real estate should be considered deftly, as buying real estate today is a great way to look toward tomorrow.

While you may think that international real estate investing is not for you, this could be a mechanism to get you moving on your feelings about getting out of the country. Many people feel that international real estate is impossible and something that they could never be involved with; however, if people realize that anything is possible and if you have always wanted to build a cottage in Holland for you to raise sheep on in your retirement, so that your wife can knit sweaters and scarves, then getting into the offshore real estate game seems to make perfect sense.

There is a backlash against the homogenizing of the American suburb as people feel that they can only have so much "sameness" stuffed down their throats. So when you are looking to an offshore tax haven this is an important thing to remember; in the future there will be all that and much more. This is an excellent reason to live somewhere that is not only safe and comfortable for you and your family but also a good investment for your next-of-kin's future.

Currently, it does not look good for much of the suburban

civilization in America. Suburbs are currently overrun, crime and poverty are commonplace, and many people feel that a welfare state is upon us.

One good thing about this sameness is that people now have choices all over the world; they can live somewhere that has rich history and culture as well as Big Macs and Frappuccinos. So that is what they are beginning to do; people reject being told what they have to do and have begun to live where the best real estate exists; where crime and repression are absent. According to one source, the population pressures are currently disseminating to the point where the environment and businesses are discouraged due to being hindered by legislation. This should be a wake-up call to anybody who feels as though the government is ineffective and who wants to change his or her life for the better in another country.

The ability to carry on commerce anywhere in the world and the ability for people to move freely from nation to nation without fear of reprisal makes the facts appealing. There are few "border struggles" or "turf wars" anymore in most civilized nations; rather, foreign nations welcome the disaffected nationals who want to live in their countries, spend money, and inject life to otherwise flat economies.

This fact is further exacerbated by the truth that people are now able to make money anywhere they want. Also, with the fairly common practice of converting American dollars into Euros or whatever the local currency is, people are freer than ever. It is a world economy and the world welcomes you into it.

If you have any interest in getting yourself into an offshore real estate deal, you should do so now rather than wait until the costs have been driven up exponentially. The reason many people are investing in offshore real estate today and holding onto it is twofold. Many people want to get away at some point in the future; having this property now and paying for it now makes planning for the future that much easier. However, even more than for themselves, there are speculators who are betting on the capital appreciation which will happen to many global markets. So with all of these disparate factors coming into play, the world economy is poised to go through a renaissance. Investors and residents both are ready to make money on par with something like the U.S. stock market from the 1980s.

If you have an interest in investing in something that is nearly guaranteed to appreciate over time, then real estate and the land on which it sits are two of the best bets you can find. Even after all other currency has lost its value, the value of a home and a property will always remain. This is due to the fact that there is an ever depleting amount of space for a population which continues to grow and grow. It is widely believed that it took longer than the first 9,000 years of human history for the world's population to reach one billion. In the last 150 years that number has gone up more than six times. With a population of around 6.6 billion people in the world and with a projected 3 million more by the year 2050, the world is becoming a tired place. So it serves that countries which today are underdeveloped may appear just about right for future generations. If there is a tax code in place for residents who are not going to be robbed by their government, then good for them. While no one knows what the future may hold and while all things may ultimately become equal, the likelihood that land will lose value is not great.

You need a place to start, and this is often the biggest hurdle which people have trouble overcoming. People are afraid of contacting and insulting other people; they feel like their requests are too farsighted for anyone to take seriously. But in reality this move is all about the relationships moving you forward in your financial ventures and in your life. These are the bonds you will forge with people who will become an integral part of your life. So if this is something which interests you, get out there! Find out the information, get someone on the phone, send out an email, and change your life.

Offshore Capital Investments

Capital investments are another option for future offshore investments. When you are talking about investing capital in the future, you could probably go where the present social status has not piqued. People follow positive trends and positivity is easily created once money is introduced. If you want to bring some capital into an emerging market; this is always best done for the long term. You cannot make any money off of something that is not there. While there are emerging market speculators all over the world, you should be wise in picking yours. There is always someone who is going to the far reaches of the world to try to find a place for people to be able to live and colonize and grow and flourish; most times these crusaders will want to bring others in with them to soften the blow of a failed adventure. This is the spirit of man and without this positivity and healthy outlook toward a new day, there would be less of a chance that man would be able to thrive.

There are a number of ways for you to be able to find out about offshore investments before you even set foot off home soil. If you look at mutual funds and what they are doing with emerging markets, you will be able to see areas where people are beginning to speculate and put some money; these are great places for you to pick up a piece of property which can one day become a real gold mine. Many mutual fund organizations and investment firms have offices where you can go and speak to someone about his or her candid feelings on various investment issues. This would be a good idea for the person who is thinking of investing overseas before he or she plants all hopes and dreams and money in any one place. If you speak to a wide variety of investment professionals, they may be able to help you come up with a better plan. You can accumulate information and then pick and choose which you want to hold onto and which to discard.

Offshore Banking

When you are living in another country and you are trying to set up your life style, you need to be able to continue living. Just because you are living in another part of the world does not mean you need to stop buying things or you will be able to get by on your good looks alone. While credit cards and other things have changed the dynamic of international commerce, when you are living in another country you should get a checking account. Opening an offshore checking account is done easily, but it will vary from country to country, so you should be sure you know what you are doing. Before you go into the bank, you should determine what paperwork and documentation you may need.

Improved communications and the advent of the computer have changed the landscape of offshore banking dramatically. Offshore banking is now a quick and inexpensive option for foreign investment opportunities as well as many other benefits.

There are many dramatic images which are brought forth when talking about offshore banking and offshore bank accounts: drug smuggling from Panama, FBI raids in Miami, or perhaps federal agents in hot pursuit of stolen briefcases full of money which has been withdrawn from a Swiss bank account. Frankly, to some these images may seem frightening. However, none of these creations have to do with the aims of this book: private and legal offshore bank accounts to save on taxes. This is an important item to remember when you are making this decision.

Offshore bank accounts allow you a great deal of freedom and mobility in your travels. One thing an offshore bank allows you to do is make investments in mutual funds and foreign stocks that are not registered by the U.S. government. You should find out any fees you would incur per transaction to see if the savings would yield a better result than what you are doing right now; chances are it will be.

Once you have a foreign bank account, you can do many different things that would not otherwise be available to you in a domestic bank account. If you have a money market account in a U.S. institution, some of these options would only be available to you with the added price tag of federal taxes. Many of the most profitable things you can do from a foreign bank account involve the purchase and sale of stocks and mutual funds, the purchase of foreign real estate, interest rates on properties in foreign countries, and profiting from fluctuations in the currency.

When you are using an offshore bank account, it allows you a certain amount of shielding from potential seizure of assets; typically, people who are looking to collect against your assets would not know about a foreign bank account up front. While they would be able to find out about it ultimately, this would require a separate action from a judge and a court in the country where the funds are located. When that happens, you will have time to combat this by moving your assets out of that account into another country.

Offshore banks operate in a completely different way from banks in the United States. Many times when a foreign bank folds, which is rare, other major banks in the country will take over the business which will ensure the depositors never lose access to funds. As a general rule, offshore bank accounts are exponentially safer than their domestic counterparts.

Offshore banks are also much more private than banks in the United States. Even with the recent changes in a country like Switzerland which used to have the pinnacle of privacy, they still far outshine the trends in the domestic American front. While the banks in the United States have done a great job in stepping up to the task of identity theft and other such travesties, there is little comparison between European banks and American banks in terms of privacy and security.

Still, the preferred method by most foreign banks for opening accounts is to go straight into the branch and meet with your banker. In general, this is the way most offshore banks do things although sometimes they may allow you to open an account through the mail. However, most foreign banks prefer to see someone in person so they know they are not doing business with a shady character.

When you are considering how you do business with banks, it should be noted that most banks allow business to be done by mail, fax, or telex. While there are some offshore banks that are gradually adding the Internet to their roster of services, most offshore banks shy away from the online world to maintain privacy.

When you open an account, you should not begin adding to the account through a domestic checking account. If there is a way for anybody to trace how the money got to that foreign bank, then that defeats the purpose of the privacy which foreign banks allow. For this reason, bringing cash into the branch is one of the best ways to make your initial deposit. There are other forms of money transfer which can be used such as a personal check, a certified check, a money order, wire transfer, a credit card transfer, or a debit card transfer, but these can all be traced back in one manner or another. So if you are looking for the privacy of foreign banks, you should consider a different way to get your money there.

One of the caveats to the U.S. law is the illegality of moving more than $10,000 in cash (or the equivalent) out of the country without filing an appropriate form. Whether you are talking about actual cash, traveler's checks, bonds, or any other securities, the law is fairly explicit. The maximum penalty for failure to report this money is five years in jail and a $500,000 fine.

If you are considering taking less than $10,000 and moving in on server vacations, there is new legislation against money laundering which outlaws manipulating the transaction to avoid your reporting this form. While you may think the first law was excessive, the money laundering law is even more stringent: a prison sentence of 20 years with no possibility for probation for first-time offenders as well as forfeiture of all of your property. Federal judges are not even allowed to hear evidence; there is no discretion in the manner in which this statute holds up in court. You can be guilty of laundering your own money; there have already been a number of legitimate convictions for less. Even if your motive is innocent and has nothing to do with any illegal activity or other manipulation, avoiding reporting is avoiding reporting and it will be treated as such.

Wire transfers are just as cumbersome. Because the federal government is looking for money wired into and out of the country by criminals, drug dealers, and terrorist supporters, there is a complicated set of rules which the banks must follow and paperwork which must be filled out. Cost has also gone up exponentially for wire transfers, making it an ineffective way to send any amount of money to most places.

Perhaps the best way to send your money anywhere is through personal check. Yes, there will still be a trail back to your name, but considering all the other problems which transferring money into and out of this country and other countries comes with, it may make a little bit more sense to do it through a personal check. If you open a separate personal or business checking account with which to fund your foreign account, that may be an even better way to go. As such, you can shut down this new account once you have drained all the funds, and when you shut down the account, the records will go into a bank's inactive file rather than on their mainframe computer. Information from this inactive file will be destroyed.

Another option is to use a domestic money market fund. Personal check writing comes with many money market funds. Once you have drained funds from this account to your new foreign account, you may close down the money market fund while it is still in your name. Getting the records from a money market fund is more difficult to do.

Believe it or not, there are reporting requisites within your foreign bank account. Big Brother wants to be everywhere in the United States and that even means in your foreign bank account. If you have a foreign bank account of $10,000 or more then you must report it. If, at any point in the year, this amount goes above $10,000, then you need to report it. And because you have to use the Federal Reserve Bank of New York's exchange rates in your calculations — these rates are only printed at the end of the year — you have a couple of options. One of the easiest things to do is distribute your wealth to your family. As long as everybody stays below the $10,000 equivalent in the foreign country, you should be fine. You should leave yourself a healthy enough margin so you do not go anywhere near $10,000. If you do go near $10,000 then you need to report it at the end of the year.

One other route for you to take to avoid the $10,000 threshold is to begin investing some of your wealth. As long as you are investing foreign stocks, bonds, mutual funds, or investment funds which are not connected to a bank account, then you should be all right.

One of the most common punishments for Americans living overseas with this $10,000 threshold is having their passport revoked. This can present numerous problems as you can be immediately flushed from your country and be brought back to the United States to be put before a judge. You should be sure to have all the rules straight before you do anything and you should know what you need to do and what you are getting yourself into before you go.

Offshore business can be a slippery slope to go down and a tough course to reverse. However, people and businesses have the need and desire to do what is necessary for their bottom line.

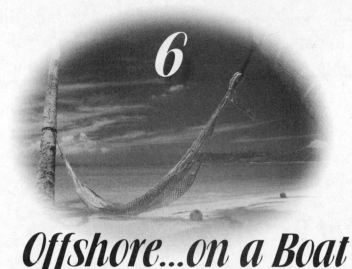

Offshore...on a Boat

Many people are unaware of how potentially altered their lives could be if they engage in an offshore tax haven. They think they will just buy a home in a quiet neighborhood on a residential street and that will be that. They will live out the rest of their lives the same as they always have. This is not the case. So to introduce the idea of an offshore tax haven, one of the most visceral examples is living on a boat.

To some, the idea of spending their whole life on the wavy waters of an ocean may seem ludicrous, but it is not as far-fetched as it may sound. The truth is that many people are able to take huge chunks of their lives and spend it on the open seas. Why not? For the fully self-reliant individual and for someone who has any experience on the water, enjoying their time on a boat may seem like the only logical conclusion.

With many ports offering you temporary harbor, some of the most breathtaking sunsets imaginable, and all the fish you can catch for your dinner, there are many fine reasons for folks who appreciate the sea to consider shoving off.

However there are also ports who will tax you if you come anywhere near them. For example, if you subsist anywhere within 12 nautical miles of the shore of the United Kingdom then you are subject to the taxes of the Queen. There are other areas of the high seas where this is true as well. While there are some ports that you can dock in for a period of days or weeks, if you overstay your welcome you will be taxed.

On the Water: On an Island?

While all this nonsense may seem problematic for some, for others it is an opportunity to band together. Perfect fodder for a reality television show, the idea of an "offshore community" has recently sprung up and taken hold of the collective imagination. Imagine an entire town, set in the middle of the ocean, on a mobile platform. The world is made up of 70 percent water, with the majority of that belonging to our oceans. That said, an idea like living on the water is plausible. On this mobile platform would be homes, shops, theatres, restaurants, and more; people would always be traveling the globe, in international waters.

Before you let Simon Cowell get his paws on this rather pure notion and try to run for king of this town, consider a few things. For one, the idea that your home country would allow you to be declared a nonresident, when you do not "actually" live anywhere, poses the first challenging obstacle. Also, you need to wonder if a town full of strangers could all successfully work together. To see evidence of this as a failed endeavor, one need look no further than prime-time network television. Unless these people were of the same mind, there is always the likelihood that someone will try to take over. Reality television, again, should show us that there is always one individual who feels he or she should be the leader.

Cruising Together

If you are interested in going global and want to spread your water wings, there are a couple of ships currently making their way into and out of ports all over the world. These are known as "residential cruise ships" and you should see about the particular stipulations of these ships. The stipulations will vary depending on how you conduct your business while on the ship and whether or not you have a mobile office of some kind or if your profits will be from investments only.

On residential cruise ships, you buy a cabin and renounce your citizenship and that is it. You can travel in perpetuity. You need to follow the proper procedures if you find a spot you would like to stay and "live." But you have complete and total freedom to live your life as you wish. However, you should always come armed with the proper information before you make any final decisions.

There is one source in particular which seems to have a great deal of insight into residential cruise ships and that is the "Halogen Guides." They can get you started on your search; they are often quoted in the *Wall Street Journal*, *Forbes*, and *Newsweek*, among others. They also have a Web site where you can subscribe to their newsletter and learn much more: **www.heliumreport.com.**

Cruising Solo

One final, more plausible alternative for the wealthy is to buy their own yacht. Yachts are available in all price categories but you should want to be comfortable, have everything you need, and have some amount of funds as a safety net in the event that anything goes wrong.

Owning a yacht is quite prestigious and will allow you the water wings to shove off and do the things you would like to do while still being able to retain your tax-free status. You would need to sell off all your territorial possessions or cleverly store them so that they could not be misconstrued as your willingness to return to terra firma one day. You would also need to keep moving so you are not classified as a "resident" in any one place.

As the frustration with taxes and ineffectual government rises, the likelihood of people taking to the open water continues to grow. One spot perfect for people trying out the nautical lifestyle is the Caribbean. With a cluster of islands within 25 miles of each other, the islands of the Caribbean are not only close but many of these territories allow visitors to stay for up to three months at a time on a tourist visa. As will be discussed in the ensuing pages, many of the islands of the Caribbean do not have any taxes; so if you decide you like it so much that you want to stay, the tax implications would not be a disadvantage.

Offshore Without Leaving Shore

Two of the most obvious tax havens are two which may not immediately come to mind. When you think of an offshore tax haven you may think of an exotic island destination or a faraway country where the language is different, the culture is different, and where you are completely apart from everything familiar. However, many people do not even consider Canada and the United States.

The healthy thing about the candidate for this manner of offshore tax haven is that, if you are currently a U.S. resident, you do not need to give up your citizenship. While it may not be complete tax avoidance, it is an encouraging steppingstone to going global in the world tax scene.

Canada

Canada is a great place to begin your offshore tax haven search for a number of reasons. First, it has been voted the best place to work and live in the world. While many cynical American citizens may not understand what is so great about Canada, the proof is in the way that the tax laws are structured.

The Canadian government says that any new Canadian citizens or immigrants may live for up to five years in Canada without taxing their non-Canadian-based income or assets. You should, of course, talk to a professional before you make any move to Canada but one wise choice, depending on your situation, may be for you to protect your assets via a trust or a corporation prior to making the move northward. This is of particular interest if you are a world investor, wealthy, a business owner, or have a business plan in a qualifying trade which will provide employment to Canadian citizens. This also is helpful if you are employed by a qualifying Canadian business which brokers in international financial centers like Montréal.

You can also get citizenship in Canada without much difficulty. If you are a U.S. resident, you should first try to see if you have any ancestry claims in Canada. You may find out you are the last surviving member of an unclaimed Canadian fortune. Then moving up to Canada would not only be beneficial for you and a tax avoidance, but you also would be able to claim your family's stagnant treasure. Of course, this is just an idea, but it is a fun one to consider.

Your world assets will be untaxed by Canada for the first five years, so if you are a U.S. citizen you should move your assets offshore and protect them from the high capital gains and income taxes with an offshore trust or a corporation before you move to Canada.

Once that initial five-year period has expired, you are no longer living in a tax shelter. If you are a nonresident, you can stay 183 days per year, but otherwise you will be subject to taxes.

A couple of notes about Canada: one thing many people may not be fully aware of is there is a continuous permafrost in the north which presents many obstacles toward development. So if you meet someone who wants to try to sell you cheap land up north, you should approach them with caution. There are also cyclonic storms east of the Rocky Mountains which produce most of the country's rain and snow east of the mountains.

More than half of the country of Canada speaks English with French coming in at nearly 25 percent. There are more unpaved airports (852) in Canada than paved airports (505), so you should be sure you know where you are touching down if you are entering the country via airplane.

Another good thing about Canada for U.S. residents is that most of the major cities in Canada — Ottawa, Calgary, Vancouver, Winnipeg, London, Toronto, and Montréal — are all near the United States' northern border. To that end, it is not difficult to cross the line and go back and forth if you want to do that.

United States

Many people may not believe it, but the United States is actually an offshore tax haven. For people who are residents of the United States and pay the excessive taxes which are charged here all the time, they may think it is just a dream. However there are numerous ways for the savvy investor and businessperson — or any individual — to avoid paying taxes and still live in the United States.

If you are coming in from outside of the United States you should know about the many different problems which could plague you once you are there. There are natural disasters such as volcanoes, earthquakes, hurricanes, tornadoes, mudslides, forest fires, flooding, and, in northern Alaska, permafrost.

There are also many social and political feuds — some of which you hear about all the time and some that you do not hear as much about on the nightly news. Among these are undocumented nationals from Mexico and Central America; boundary disputes with Canada at the Dixon entrance; the U.S. naval base at Guantánamo Bay; Haiti's claims to the U.S.-administered Navassa Island; war in Iraq and Afghanistan; hostility toward Iran, Syria, Palestine, North Korea, and Pakistan; prolonged drought; overrun population growth; an outdated water-sharing program with Mexico; and the fact that the United States has made no territorial claim in Antarctica and does not recognize the right of any other country to do so.

With all of these problems going on, you would think that the United States would be a horrible place to live. But nothing could be further from the truth. Despite the fact that the United States has some of the biggest problems in the world as well as some of the highest taxes, it also has some of the best medical treatment facilities, police protective services, cultural institutions, educational institutions, public services, and anything else you can imagine.

Examine New York City. With 8.2 million people living in a 322-square-mile area, it is the gateway from the east. It has with two major airports, two local professional baseball teams, a single arena that becomes a basketball court, hockey arena, and concert hall all in the same week; 39 Broadway theaters, hundreds of off-Broadway theaters, and uncounted off-off Broadway theaters; a litany of shopping, tourist, and special-event things going on in addition to the thousands of restaurants and thousands of hotels; what more could you be looking for? But enough about my hometown — let me just say that the United States offers a great deal of things to see and enjoy.

So if you are looking for tax breaks in the United States and you are trying to find a way to make it work for yourself, you may wish to consider looking into the Nevada Limited Liability Companies, partnerships, and trusts. Nevada-based companies and partnerships are exempt from U.S. taxes for a number of reasons. These include income earned outside of the United States, gains from sale of shares of corporate stock, non-U.S. interest and dividends, U.S. Bank interest, income from U.S. imports (if no sales office is located inside of the United States), and income from U.S. exports (if no sales office is located inside the United States).

This may seem like it is particular and exclusive, but one of the nicest things about the Nevada Limited Liability

Company agreement is that the company does not have to file a U.S. tax return or pay U.S. income tax.

Another great thing you can participate in is U.S. trusts. These can gain tax exemption on gains from the sale of shares of a corporate stock, foreign-source interest and dividends, and U.S. Bank interest.

To live in the United States tax-free, do not overstay your welcome of 153 days. This is shorter than many of the other countries in the world. The only exclusion is if you are a Canadian citizen, in which case you are allowed to stay here for up to one year, with a one-year extension.

While many people in the general populace of the United States may not believe they are eligible for tax-free status within their own country, there are ways for you to skirt around many of the tax traps we all fall into. You should speak to a professional if you plan on staying inside the United States, because being audited for tax evasion comes with a new set of penalties which do not take the individual situation into account. This is a definite push to get people to stop trying to do this, and it should be discouraging unless you are sure you are playing by the rules.

8

Island Escapes: Reliable Tax Havens

This list is in no way meant to be composite or exclusionary; you should always speak with a tax professional or tax preparer or lawyer of some kind who specializes in this sort of thing before you make the move into any particular area, as change is happening all of the time. However, these listed areas have had a great deal of success and they continue to be favorites of the tax avoider.

As these are all island nations, they have significant benefits and drawbacks which will be discussed individually. In short, your resources are the skill and product of what lies on the island; if there are no neurologists, helicopters, public parks, or paved roads, then that is it. While the drawbacks to these tax siestas need to be kept in mind, for the most part these regions have been receptive to people seeking a tax-free existence.

Many people may wonder why these otherwise wonderful tourist destinations are tax-free societies. They are islands, which make foreign invasion highly unlikely; this thereby all but eliminates a defense budget. And with an ethnically mixed populace and virtually no racial friction or other crime issues, their police forces are blissfully complacent.

To some people, the idea of a complacent police force is like a scene out of a George Orwell novel; if this is you, you probably should not consider these island nations. Furthermore, the technological innovations of the last 50 years may be absent. While there are telephones, televisions, Internet, and washing machines, people live a much simpler existence and view much of these advancements as little more than the buzz of modern life.

Many of the no-tax havens discussed in this section have a British colonial background and are members of the Commonwealth. These smaller Commonwealth countries still use the imperialist tradition from 19th-century Britain, which excluded all local taxation. This is good news for people who are considering moving there for a tax-free existence, as the legal tradition is that common law is not corrupted by socialist legislation. The official language on all of the Commonwealth islands is English, which is another boon for the English-speaking expatriate.

These countries have been tax-free for many years and have a big stake in staying that way. For both the tradition and the practicality of the matter, there is little to fear when it comes to change. The cynic in us all may be thinking to himself or herself, "Yeah, 300 years and then they are going to start taxing as soon as I get off the boat!" While this is unlikely, you can consult with your tax professional to learn all the details.

Perhaps the biggest difficulty for living in any of these areas is the difficulty finding a reason to establish incorporation there. When any outside observer sees the Bahamas, the Cayman Islands, or Bermuda, their vision immediately goes to tax evasion. There are other things about these areas which could further complicate their nontaxability and make them seem like something that might not be as good a fit for everybody as first appears. However, these areas are ones which should be considered; so let us further investigate and try to find out where they fit into your offshore tax haven philosophy.

American Samoa

The irony is not lost that in a book written by an American citizen, for release by an American publisher, in many American marketplaces, the first island escape would actually be an American territory. But it is true that American Samoa offers many of the benefits of domestic life, yet has a much lower cost of living.

American Samoa has a tropical marine climate which is moderated by the trade winds. They have a rainy season from November to April and a dry season from May to October with little seasonal temperature variation. While this may make some people who have previously lived in desert areas like Los Angeles or Arizona uncomfortable, it is an easy thing to get used to.

With a good communication structure in place you can do a lot of business on the American Samoa islands and enjoy yourself. You do not even have to exchange your currency as they use the American dollar and, with the three airports to get into and out of the island, you can almost always find somebody who is willing to take you somewhere for the right price.

Language may be a bit of a challenge on American Samoa as many people there speak Samoan. Samoan is a Polynesian language which is closely related to Hawaiian. They also speak English on American Samoa and most people are bilingual. But if you are going to be dealing with all types of people, then you should be familiar with the language so you are not at a disadvantage when you are dealing with some of the locals.

The main industries include tuna canneries and handicrafts. The one major disadvantage of being way out on American Samoa is that you are in Oceania, which is approximately midway between Hawaii and New Zealand in the South Pacific Ocean. Things cost a lot more to get to where you are and, even though the stability of the social structure is in place, you need to remember that you are subjected to things such as typhoons, which are common between December and March.

If you can stand the reclusiveness though, American Samoa is just as good a place as any in the Caribbean to have your offshore tax haven. In fact, with all the great distance that people have to travel to get to where you are, especially if you are looking to be away from people for a while, American Samoa may just be the place to go.

Anguilla

A little-known country that many people have never even heard of in the northeastern Caribbean is Anguilla. A British overseas territory which is only 16 miles long, Anguilla is known for its beaches, excellent temperatures, and low rainfall.

If you are interested in just relaxing on the beach, then this place is right for you. As far as a tax haven, Anguilla has no income tax, no inheritance or other estate tax, no capital gains tax, no gift tax, and no corporation tax, making it one of the best bets for anybody who is interested in escaping the clutches of the tax man.

Anguilla is an ideal spot for the person who wants to move overseas, lead a relaxed life style, and will be living off of investments. Setting up a trust in Anguilla is also a good idea. More often than not, people like doctors or lawyers, who are subject to negligence claims, will set up what is known as an asset protection trust to shield themselves from lawsuits. There is only one area where people could get in trouble with their trust in Anguilla, and this is when you are talking about a divorce, debt, or overseas taxes; otherwise this country's respect for privacy and secrecy is paramount.

If people are afraid of moving their assets to an overseas area, they should be reassured that Anguilla is under British rule; also, for Americans who are afraid of putting their money with a name that they are not familiar with, there are well-respected American banks that have branches in Anguilla, including Bank of America. Another advantage for people who are unfamiliar with the area is the low crime rate; it is one of the lowest in the world.

There are some things which may turn people off when they are looking at this island as a potential tax haven. One of the problems is that foreigners cannot buy beachfront property in the beach island community. While other properties are relatively low in price — a three- or four-bedroom property close to the beach for $200,000 to $300,000 — the foreign investor will need to pay a 12.5 percent property transfer tax.

Obtaining residence in Anguilla can also be something of a challenge. To maintain permanent residence on the island, you need to buy a property and then apply for a certificate. If you are interested in working on the island, you will need to be able to get a permit. As is typical of most Caribbean tax havens, getting a work permit is difficult, as the authorities are reluctant to issue them to people who may be taking jobs away from residents. However, if you will be bringing work to the island or if you will be working in a specialized field it may be a little bit easier.

Antigua and Barbuda

Antigua and Barbuda is a place where many of the locals are trying to lure offshore tax haven seekers by levying no personal income taxes and no export taxes unless you are exporting any of the local fare, such as Sea Island cotton, sugar, molasses, fish, or lobster.

Another benefit to trying to set up a corporation in Antigua and Barbuda is that while they ring up a 40 percent corporation tax on incorporated companies, as well as a 2 percent tax on incorporated companies if you are not planning on doing a great deal of business, you do not need to worry about that. The reason is that the first $4,166 of your gross income in any calendar month is exempt from corporation taxes. This means if you want to just do the bare minimum and earn less than that amount of money, you can be tax free. If you own commercial property, you will pay .75 percent on your taxable income unless your property is a hotel where you will pay .20 percent.

With a fairly good communications system and little temperature variation in the lateral climate, Antigua and Barbuda is a great place to go. They have three airports, English is the official language, and with the main industry of tourism you may just see somebody you used to know from your old job back where you were getting taxed. With a predominance of Anglican Christians, the religious climate is not varied but the stable political and social climates make for a great place to call home and your tax-free life.

Anjouan

A restrictive place for many, Anjouan is a tiny Sunni Muslim island in the middle of the Indian Ocean which has many tax benefits, but also many health concerns. The GDP is around $700 and thus it is one of the world's poorest countries. There are a number of mosques, the people there are embroiled in a perpetual civil war, and the tap water is not safe to drink. Alcohol is illegal, mosquitoes carrying malaria are abundant, and the literacy of the women on the island is said to be less than 60 percent.

You may ask yourself what could possibly be the reason you would want to establish an offshore tax shelter there. Well, if you are considering registration of a ship or aircraft, the laws in this country are extremely lax. Also, if you are interested in opening up a gambling company, the licenses are quite easy to get.

There are further stipulations, such as you need to pay a hefty fee to be granted a banking license (to get a bank account), and even though they are a developing nation, the radio, Internet, and phone services are still being developed. But with a 0 percent corporate tax rate, if you are a Muslim and you are looking for a place to establish an offshore business, Anjouan may be the place for you.

Aomen Tebie Xingzhengqu (Macau Special Administrative Region)

There are a number of spots in the South Pacific Ocean and near China which are perfect spots for Chinese citizens or for Hong Kong businesses. Just because of the individual islands which litter the South Pacific and because of the fact that everybody wants to get up on the same level in terms of economic development, many regions grant forgiveness for tax burdens to spurn on the economic development. One of these regions is Aomen Tebie Xingzhengqu or what is known as the Macau Special Administrative Region.

As a small trio of islands extending from Macau on the south shores of China, these areas are perfect for people who are looking to incorporate an offshore business and for what is known as a Macau Offshore Company (MOC). The social climate is stable and there is a subtropical marine climate which is subjected to some typhoons, but only seasonally.

If you are looking to form an offshore business in this region then you have options. Just be sure that you are not depending on a large manufacturing facility or other delicate, weather-sensitive structure. You should also be wary because you cannot sell your service or your product to any Macau residents or trade in the Macau market. Other than that, you will be able to trade virtually tax free. You should consult with a specialist in Macau for further details, but as a budding area for the offshore tax shelter this is an area of the world which deserves your scrutiny.

Aruba

Aruba is one of the more pleasant places to stay if you are seeking an offshore tax haven status in the West Indies. With a great number of things to do, pleasant weather for the most part, and an idyllic setting in general, Aruba is a perfect place to run your business from, recruit locals, invest your money, and live tax free. Associated with the Dutch government, Aruba is a free trade zone which has a 0 percent corporate tax and a 0 percent personal income tax.

If you are interested in staying in Aruba, there are many things there for you to do. There is a great mix of religion although particularly pointed is the Roman Catholic percentage, though there are Protestant, Hindu, Muslim, Confucian, and Jewish disciplines as well, making Aruba a well-rounded religious society. And with absolutely zero international disputes, Aruba is a stable place to live and to enjoy your tax-free status.

If you are a nonresident of the island of Aruba, you can stay 90 days if you are not a Dutch citizen and 180 days if you are Dutch. There is a 14-day stay for visa holders though a visa is not required for U.S., EU, and Canadian nationals. If you wish to enjoy a longer stay, there are temporary residence permits but they are restricted in that you cannot compete for jobs with Aruba nationals. There are no restrictions on any real estate purchases you may wish to make.

Australia

As you will come to see, we will be discussing many offshore tax havens located in Oceania in the South Pacific Ocean which are located around the much larger nations of New Zealand and Australia. But for good measure, it is worth discussing Australia briefly.

If you are looking for a place to stay and you do not need to conduct any business, then Australia may be one of the ports that you would wish to consider. With an excellent social climate, communications network, many airports, strong economy, activities, tourist destinations, and temperate climate, Australia is a great place to visit and a great place to call home temporarily.

However, if you are looking for a place to call home permanently, Australia comes with many of the shackles that many of the larger nations of the world do. If you incorporate in Australia, have your company's central management set up there, if you carry out your business there, or even if you have Australians who are allowed voting rights within your company, you will be subjected to all of the nation's excessive corporate taxes.

Two easy ways to help avoid this is to make sure you do not carry out your business there and that you do not stay more than 183 days per year. Due to the fact that Australia has a well-run local government, you should also try to maintain your privacy concerning any offshore financial or business activities you have. They are likely to want to dabble in that when they are able to, so you should use discretion. Also, the nonresident stay can get a little bit complicated if you begin to get near the 183 days a year in consecutive years, so you should be wary of your dates because once you have become victim to the personal tax known as the inland revenue, it is difficult for you to remedy.

Azores

As an unspoiled and well-connected island area well off of the mainland shores of Portugal, the Azores is a winter tourist retreat which still remains connected to mainland Europe through its series of well-maintained airports all over the islands. Similarly, for the well-connected people on the island as well as the expatriate seeking an offshore tax haven, there are other good systems of communications put in place.

The Azores are an ideal spot for the offshore worker with a mobile office who is able to generate all of his or her income from another source. Similarly, if you are a well-endowed individual and are simply looking to live off of your own wealth and love life, then the Azores may just be your launching pad. With its proximity to everywhere from its perch in the middle of nowhere, the Azores islands are a place for you to be at once nearby and at the same time miles away from everything.

If you are looking for work though, you are a lot more likely to find your sustenance elsewhere. Most of the industry on the island is limited to things such as sugar refining and liquor distilling. Due to its subtropical climate and up-and-coming status, the gambling entrepreneur may wish to open up a small bed-and-breakfast there, but the Azores is not known for tourism. If you are considering moving there, you should be aware that there is a pronounced rainy season from November to March and all year long the temperature is more humid than not.

The Bahamas

Composed of 700 islands and rocks and reefs; stretching from Haiti to Florida, this tax haven is a classic one. With a total land area of 5,400 square miles over 70,000 square miles of ocean, the Bahamas was one of the first tax havens. Full of sun, sand, fun, and relaxed tourists, the Bahamas seems like a utopia. With miles of tranquil ocean over which people are boating, laughing, and having a great time, the Bahamas may be the end for many who never want to leave. With an average minimum of 70 degrees Fahrenheit and an average maximum of 80 degrees, the Bahamas is a weather utopia.

In terms of their economy, the Bahamas relies primarily on tourism, though they do engage in a few domestic exports, including petroleum, rum, cement, and salt.

The Bahamas are fairly accessible by plane from major destinations all over the world, including London, Toronto, and major American cities; from Miami these islands are a short flight of just around half an hour.

Even though 50 percent of the total population of the Bahamas is found on one island, there are a host of services that are available; banks, law firms, finance companies, accountants, and others are available en masse. Many of these services and service providers are the perfect answer for the no-tax, haven-seeking individual.

And when you are talking about taxes, they do not exist in the Bahamas. There is no personal income tax, no corporate tax, no profit tax, and no estate or death tax; in short, no taxes. The government makes most of its money from the local casinos, and there is a small tax on the increase in value when you make improvements to your land.

Bahrain

With the current political climate in the Middle East, many people may wish to stay away from this area of the world. However, there is one place where there is a predominance of Shi'a and Sunni Muslim religion and, despite that fact, the country is relatively stable. This country is prosperous and offers a wide array of tax advantages to do business in the Middle East. With international banking and with all kinds of tax breaks for nonresidents seeking to do business there, Bahrain has asserted itself as a leader in the progressive, forward-thinking Middle Eastern policy.

With a strong position in a number of industries, including petroleum processing, petroleum refining, offshore banking, ship repair, aluminum smelting, as well as tourism, Bahrain has established itself as an excellent spot just east of Saudi Arabia in the Middle East and the Persian Gulf.

While many Westerners may have a negative impression of what goes on in the Middle East and a feeling that everyone in Arabic countries is either rich or poor, the GDP in Bahrain in 2003 was estimated at $18.02 million and they have an excellent communication system among other things. Even though Arabic is the official language, English is spoken and understood in most areas and especially for business purposes.

Barbados

While Barbados is a lovely destination in the Caribbean Sea, the corporate tax is troubling. The situation in Barbados is that they have a high, complex corporate tax rate.

If you are a nonresident of Barbados, you may stay there are 180 days per year and you can avoid all your tax on personal income as there is a 0 percent personal tax for nonresidents. But you need to watch out how long you stay there every year, because if you are classified as a resident then your world income will be taxed for the entire year.

With principal industries in sugar, light manufacturing, component assembly, as well as tourism, Barbados is an English-speaking island which is a lovely place to stay and should be considered if you are doing some traveling in your tax-free life.

Bermuda

Many American expatriates move to Bermuda to avoid tax later on in life. Bermuda is close to the United States and it offers a high standard of living. It also has a nice climate and English is the official language on the island although many people do speak Portuguese. There are hurricanes which are liable to occur from June to November and there are strong winds which do kick up in the winter time. But otherwise it has nice weather.

It is also a great place to carry out your business if you are not recruiting Bermudian staff. If you recruit Bermudian people to work for you then you may have to pay payroll and social taxes. The only way you can apply for citizenship is if you are married to a Bermudian citizen for over 10 years and then apply. You can only buy a house if you pay 22 percent of the cost of the property to the government. Expatriate long-term residency is limited to six years.

You can live on the island as a nonresident for considerably longer than on most others. You will be subject to 0 percent personal taxes as long as your income is not derived locally.

With a stable social climate, Bermuda would be the perfect place for you to live and play.

British Virgin Islands

To take advantage of the tax allowances afforded residents of the British Virgin Islands you need to be aware of the rules. You need to be a citizen, first of all, and this may be more challenging than you would think. One of the quickest ways is to get married to a local citizen. As long as you marry one of the citizens of the British Virgin Islands, that is fine with them.

Another way to get resident status in the British Virgin Islands is by investing a large sum of money. Another way to gain resident status in the British Virgin Islands is by investing a large sum of money to the tune of $250,000 into local property By investing this amount of money, the British Virgin Islands sees that you are interested in staying for the long term or are at least interested in giving something back to the community, and will therefore grant you residence status. If you do not have either of these, you cannot stay past your six months or you will be subjected to your world income being taxed at the British Virgin Islands tax rate in addition to the taxes levied by your home country.

Brunei Darussalam

An area in southeast Asia that has shown much improvement in recent years is Brunei Darussalam. Brunei is one of the nations which offers some of the best medical care and education in the world. With flourishing economic opportunities and numerous operational and tax benefits for investors, this is a perfect place for the disillusioned Asian citizen or just somebody who wants to break out of a shell and try something totally different.

Despite the fact that Malay is their official language, Chinese and English are also regularly spoken. As long as you are willing to deal with a little bit of challenge at first, any halfway-educated American citizen or English-speaking citizen should be able to get acclimated quickly.

There is also a stable social climate in this region of the world; in 2003, Brunei and Malaysia ceased their exploration for offshore oil and gasoline, resolved their disputes over regions which were once in contention, and went on to a fairly peaceful existence.

For the investor, there are a number of popular reasons for you to consider moving your funds over to Brunei. There are a number of popular banks which have set up shop in this small nation, including Hong Kong Bank, Islamic Bank of Brunei, Standard Chartered Bank, and Citibank. Unfortunately any American citizen who is looking to escape their Citibank credit card bills will have to find a different offshore tax shelter to escape to.

Brunei also offers something known as the Dedicated Cell Companies (DCC), which has also been known as the Protected Cell Companies. This is a structure that allows an investor to segregate assets into subsidiaries so that creditors and lawsuits can only affect an associate subsidiary and not the whole company. Hopefully your business will never be subject to lawsuits, but as any good business owner knows, there are often things which are out of your control and which happened despite your best efforts to the contrary.

Canary Islands

With a consistent temperature and a great number of attractive benefits, the Canary Islands are a great place for you to set up your offshore tax haven. Because of their association with the European Union, many people consider the Canary Islands to be just another British colony. However, the EU levies no VAT (Value Added Tax) or duty on special capital increases and offers many tax advantages for trading with Spain.

The Canary Islands are popular for people looking to establish a second home or have a retirement somewhere completely off the beaten path. Located just southwest of Spain, northwest of Africa, and right in front of the coast of Morocco, the Canary Islands are a perfect place for people to enjoy steady temperatures and beautiful conditions all year round.

The weather is touted as only fluctuating within six degrees throughout the entire year; so many people who are looking for a place to call home will find this enticing.

Cayman Islands

Many individuals from the United States or Canada find their way down to the Cayman Islands when they are first considering their offshore tax haven reality. They are close, they are a UK territory, and there is a low crime rate and a high standard of living. Their political and social stability is welcoming; their official language is English, and they offer a fairly composite (and always growing) system of communications via both landlines, cellular, and Internet access. While these may seem to the younger generation like rights more than amenities, any individual who has been around for a time can remember an era before the World Wide Web and anyone who has done any international travel will be able to relay to you that sometimes leaving your own shores is like taking a step back in time.

Fortunately for the Cayman Islands, though, there is a great deal of money being put into their infrastructure with only more to follow. And fortunately for the independently wealthy among us, the Cayman Islands is a perfect spot to settle down and not seek employment. With a 0 percent income tax rate on the unemployed on the islands, there is real reason to seek your offshore tax haven out in the warm and placid waters of the Caribbean Sea.

There is also a 0 percent corporate tax rate with small administrative fees for things like stamp duties and legal paper preparation. Going right along with that, there is a 50-year tax exemption license for limited partnerships which carry on trade outside of the country, making the Cayman Islands the perfect spot for you to set up your eBay trading business. Finally, if you are interested in becoming incorporated within the Cayman Islands, there are some small fees that go along with that.

If this sounds enticing, it gets even better. You will be able to enjoy the benefits of a no-tax, nonresident existence indefinitely so long as you invest more than $180,000 into a property or local business and so long as you are not employed inside the country. This means you can finally sell that condo in Miami and hop on a plane and buy that great huge home in the middle of the ocean and carry on your off-site e-business for as long as you want and never pay taxes again.

There is the seasonal likelihood of being hit by a tropical hurricane, though. The rainy season also lasts from May to October, so if you are worried about being washed away, you may wish to consider a drier climate.

Christmas Island

While many may not even consider this tropical island in the Indian Ocean a viable offshore tax haven, it is a tax haven. As a popular place for many local Australians, this English-speaking nation has a good deal of other benefits to its inhabitants which could make it an excellent option for anyone who is interested in settling in a developing country.

The tropical climate combined with the pronounced "wet" and "dry" seasons may render Christmas Island a bit off-putting for some older folks. Also, the low GDP and their seemingly impoverished status is a bit of a hindrance for people who have lived in developed nations their whole lives. However, the island is a politically stable area and tourism is one of the biggest draws to those who are informed.

With a mix of Buddhist, Muslim, and Christian people, this could be a somewhat of a deal breaker for people who are afraid of that dynamic. However, the Muslim community is of Malaysian descent and they live in peace with the Chinese Buddhists and the Australian Christians.

If you are considering Christmas Island for an offshore tax shelter you would be wise to refrain from becoming a citizen. Christmas Island residents have Australian taxes levied against them; combine this fact with the trade tariffs you would be subject to, or if you have any trade with mainland Australia, and becoming a resident does not make a whole lot of sense.

However, one of the biggest draws to Christmas Island, for temporary guests and for investing purposes, is that there are no taxes on goods and services. So doing some offshore investing in bringing tourism to the island is always a viable option. Furthermore, if you are operating a mobile business, Christmas Island may be a good place to locate yourself in a temporary fashion. Also, if you have relocated on your ship into international waters, you could use the ports of Christmas Island during their dry seasons. You should be wary of the narrow reef which surrounds the island, as it has posed itself as a marine hazard in the past.

Cocos (Keeling) Islands

This is a small and isolated island region which presents a great opportunity for the savvy investor. Clustered together in the southeast Asian region of the Indian Ocean, this island area is not well known to many outsiders. Situated approximately halfway between Australia and Sri Lanka, the Cocos Islands present an excellent opportunity for the industrious, practicing Muslim. To reap all the benefits that this region offers, you need to understand and respect the Muslim traditions as the population is less than 700 people and they are virtually all Muslim.

Despite their use of Australian currency and being an Australian territory, the Cocos Islands represent an excellent opportunity for someone seeking a much slower pace of life. While the residents of the island are welcoming of outsiders, someone considering this area for an offshore tax haven should be wise to the fact that it is located in the middle of the Indian Ocean and he or she will be totally isolated from the rest of the world. Combine that with a small population with whom to do business and your opportunities are further constricted.

There are a number of incentives and opportunities for business growth and creation offered by the larger Australian government as they no doubt see the opportunities inherent in such a beautiful, tropical place. There is no goods or services tax on the islands and the general concessions are heightened by the Australian government.

Despite their Muslim population and their relative isolation, the people of the Cocos Islands are a peaceful bunch and their political and social stability is intact.

Cook Islands

Some benefits are worth the trouble, but not all of them. To enjoy the tax-free status on the Cook Islands there is a complicated system set up whereby if you are a nonresident you cannot buy land there, and if you are a nonresident and you want to stay longer than the 31-day tourist visa term, you need to apply for a work permit. To get a work permit, though, you need have a job; it is like the old dilemma of "how to get a job without experience?"

You cannot blame the islands for doing right by themselves, though. The Cook Islands are eager to improve their economic standing both locally and in the world. It would seem that if they were dedicated to doing good things for themselves, they would take the hard road and sell property cheaper or at least engage people who took a vested interest. It seems they are unwilling to let rich foreigners just come in and swoop up their land; therefore you need to be able to show a vested interest in staying there long term and investing your capital back into the local economy. This catch-22 allows few to come in and spoil the natural beauty of the Cook Islands.

The only exception to this rule is if you are starting a business there which will benefit the island. Your business will enjoy a small corporate tax rate of around 12.5 percent and even if you start a business there, there are all sorts of import taxes which need to be paid if you are going to bring anything from the outside. Also troubling to businesses is the tax that you pay on worldwide profits — with a nondomestic company — of 20 percent. Another troubling factor about the Cook Islands is that the GDP per capita is a paltry $5,000, making the island an unlikely place to depend on for any of your domestic riches being made.

All of these factors line up to a distressing economic forecast for someone looking to make money in the Cook Islands. If you are looking for a perfect and unspoiled place to holiday then perhaps you would wish to consider the Cook Islands; however, as an offshore tax haven, the Cook Islands may be best left alone.

Costa Rica

Cleverly situated in a volatile position in the world, tucked between Panama and Nicaragua, Costa Rica is an ideal place to base your tax haven. Costa Rica posits that there should be no tax on any overseas income, period. However, there is the caveat that any income which is earned inside of Costa Rica itself could be subject to any kind of taxation. If you are comfortable being a resident of Costa Rica, so long as any income-producing assets you have are not within the country, you have no tax payable.

There is tax on any capital gains which are earned inside of Costa Rica. Even if you are doing local trade with people, there is tax payable on this. Taxes in Costa Rica can be at local rates of up to 25 percent.

Much to the delight of the savvy investor, there are not even capital gains tax assessed in Costa Rica. If you are caught out in some manner and Costa Rican officials try to apply tax to some of your capital gains, this can be easily obfuscated by getting rid of whatever investments or property you have which would have warranted these taxes.

While the former personality of a country like Costa Rica was such that it made people a little wary of moving there, people inside of Costa Rica experience some of the best life style of anyone in Central America. And you can live there for pretty cheap. If you learn the local customs and trade, you can get local goods fairly inexpensively; the only time you are ever going to pay too much is for imported goods.

With a decent climate all year round and good communications, including telephone and Internet, Costa Rica can be a great place for you to relocate. You are going to need to protect yourself a little bit more than in the affluent areas of the United States, for example, as Central America in general has been plagued with a long tradition of crime. Still, Costa Rica is among the safest of all the Central American countries. And if you are still young or interested in living the adventurous life, or if you have found an enclave of a community within the area with which you are familiar, then you should be fine.

In general, the property prices are fairly inexpensive in Costa Rica, and there are a number of speculative investors who go to the area to take advantage of this. It would seem that a country like Costa Rica is poised to make its move into the 21st century by showing its good side to investors and future residents from the world over. It is a long time in coming and the people of Costa Rica appear to be ready for it, as it has long been touted as one of the up-and-coming hotspots in the world.

If you are looking for a bargain, then Costa Rica appears to be the place to go. With some beachfront property prices as low as $100,000, it may be a place to go for generations to come. Quality beachfront properties go for around a half-million dollars, but there are bargains to be found everywhere you look, so you should stay vigilant; when you see the property of your dreams, you should strike.

Costa Rica also has an interesting setup for people who have a guaranteed income and would like to experience the life style in Costa Rica. This scheme is known as "rentista." A prospective tenant needs to prove that he or she has at least $1,000 guaranteed monthly income for a single individual, or $2,000 for a married couple, and show that he or she has the intention to live within Costa Rica for at least six months out of the year. Once you have met both of these requirements, you are able to take advantage of the tax exemption on your non-Costa Rican income.

The tax burden on local companies can be high; but offshore companies which have seen no activity in Costa Rica and hold no assets in Costa Rica are able to avoid local taxes in full. As a vehicle for good opportunities and for individuals who are looking to break free from their home country's tax burden and establish themselves on the world stage, Costa Rica still appears to be one of the best options available.

Cyprus

If you are interested in going to a European country which will enable you to not only avoid capital gains tax, but also enable you to set up offshore structures which will be beneficial in terms of holding assets, and for investment companies, then you should consider Cyprus. Cyprus is a mere four-hour flight from the United Kingdom and is becoming an increasingly popular destination for people who want to avoid capital gains taxes and set up offshore structures.

Cyprus has a number of positive exemptions and reasons for people to consider this area as a tax haven. While there are great exemptions in many countries, the exemptions located in Cyprus are: interest received by individuals, 50 percent of interest income of companies, dividends, profits of permanent establishments carrying on a trade abroad, profits from the sale of shares, and income from employment services provided abroad to a nonresident employer. All of these are tax free, and that is the way they are intended to stay. There are also mechanisms in which people who own property and sell property in a foreign country will not be taxed at the local rate.

Particularly for the European, Cyprus is an enviable choice. People who are familiar with the style of life in Europe or who have grown up in or around Europe will be able to appreciate much of the comforts available in an area like Cyprus. Cyprus is a well-developed country with plenty of great communications and transportation alternatives, as well as a great selection of department stores, restaurants, and anything else you could want to make a home.

With a Mediterranean climate and plenty of sunshine in the spring, summer, and early fall, you can bet that Cyprus is a choice for many people who are looking for an alternative. They have a low crime rate in Cyprus, and it is fairly easy for European citizens to establish residency there.

Dubai

For individuals who are looking for a popular destination to cash in on local property and earn a tax-free salary, Dubai is an important addition to the discussion. With no personal income tax, capital gains tax, inheritance tax, or sales tax, Dubai is a country which has much to offer.

One of the other good things about Dubai as a potential place to settle is that if you want to visit Dubai, you can go there on a 14- or 30-day tourist visa. However, if you see property you like in Dubai and you want to act on impulse and just purchase it, you can do so. Once you have purchased property you will be able to apply for a residence permit, which gives you unfettered access into and out of Dubai.

While this may seem like a dream come true, the dream is not so simple. One of the things restricting the buying of property is that you are only allowed to buy property within certain zones or areas which are constricted to development and for people who are from out of the country. As a nonresident, you need to be able to buy property inside of these zones before you are able to apply for a residence permit. However, once you obtain a residence permit and you do live there, you should be able to snatch up whatever property you want.

For all of its reputation, Dubai is known as an excellent place to live and raise a family, as there are plenty of great hospitals and schools in the area. While there are alternatives for every different family, there are many international schools that are available for those raising children. Though these are going to be a lot more expensive than whatever public schools are available, they are available so you can maintain your Western traditions.

With a mix of local shopping facilities and markets, as well as impressive malls and other larger shopping facilities where there are high-tech goods, computers, all electronics, and other things for the dabbling Westerner to recall, Dubai is perfect for anyone from any life style.

Dubai is a Muslim country, although the population has been cast as high as 50 percent Westerners. You can get alcohol, and restaurants, hotels, and most people speak English even though Arabic is the official language of this country.

For people who are interested in setting up a company there, a hefty incorporation fee is imposed, and the annual or renewal fees are quite expensive as well. However, the benefit to this is a zero tax rate you would enjoy; so if you are going to be opening up a company in Dubai, you should certainly speak to somebody first to see if it would make sense for the amount of money you are going to be taking in.

Dubai is a private place, and a registered company offers a level of confidentiality which is enviable. Dubai even has a virtual place to set up a company — what is known as the Dubai Internet City. Specifically for e-commerce, this is a free-trade zone available online.

Despite the political sensitivity of the area in which Dubai is located, it could be said that Dubai is an excellent option for people interested in the offshore tax haven — particularly people who are interested in investing in property, because the returns can be great.

Federated States of Micronesia

The Federated States of Micronesia are an amalgamation of 607 islands extending 1800 miles, east of the Philippines in Oceania. Due to the fact that this is such a widespread area and that the islands themselves are so small and tribal in nature, this is one of those places in the world which may never get up to speed. They have a poor communications system despite the fact that they may seem very connected. For example, these small islands have six paved airports; however, the communication barriers run deep. While having a unified state of island nations may seem like a positive, the languages which are spoken there include English, Trukese, Pohnpeian, Yapese, Kosrean, Ulithian, Wolsaian, Nukuoro, and Kapingamarangi. This makes even the most basic communication — talking — a challenge.

Their infrastructure is such that the Federated States of Micronesia do not have access to the resources which they need to make themselves a tourist destination. While setting up an offshore tax haven in this region of the world is popular on other islands, you should speak with a tax professional before you make your way to the Federated States of Micronesia.

Their social climate is favorable toward setting up an offshore tax haven, but their rules have not caught up to the times. They have a split Roman Catholic and Protestant populace, and the only real problem with this place is that it rains practically year-round. They are in the typhoon belt as well, so the Federated States of Micronesia are subjected to errant weather patterns.

And while the Federated States of Micronesia is a free, sovereign group of states, the fact remains that they are heavily influenced by not only the United States but the United Nations, and are heavily reliant on foreign aid for just about everything. Check back with the Federated States of Micronesia in about 20 years if you are a young person reading this book, because remote territories like this could be the place where people end up going in the future.

Fiji

Fiji is a recently independent series of islands (more than 300 in total) located in the south Pacific Ocean whose principal industries include sugar, clothing, gold, silver, lumber, and tourism. While the country of Fiji does have numerous restrictions on its residents — namely that non-Fiji born residents may never own the land — it is still a beautiful place to visit and a great place for the wealthy and well endowed to enjoy a fair tax haven.

Just be aware, though, that if you are conducting business on Fiji, you will pay taxes. Fiji has an income tax of 35 percent for a resident company and 45 percent for a nonresident company, as well as a 10 percent value-added tax (VAT); so if you are doing business, one way or another you will pay taxes. However, if you are independently wealthy and are looking to relax and enjoy the beautiful scenery, then there are plenty of reasons for you to go to Fiji.

Even though you cannot own land on the island unless you are native born, you may still lease property. You should be sure to check all of the individual potential tax burdens you could be shouldering if you do make your way to Fiji, depending upon your individual situation. However, with the tropical marine climate which only has slight temperature variations, good communications, a number of airports, and a good mix of Catholic, Muslim, Hindu, and other religious beliefs, you can bet that Fiji is at the top of many people's lists when they are looking for a place to escape to.

French Polynesia

There are a number of reasons on the surface why it may appear to be a great idea to go to the French Polynesian islands. There is no income tax and even though they charge a VAT for services and goods, it never is more than 10 percent. However, there are strikes against this cluster of islands which run much deeper than low taxes.

On one of the main islands of French Polynesia, Marutoa, France had been testing nuclear bombs up until 1995.

While many may disregard the testing as old news — more than a decade old — and not to be worried about, the government agencies in charge of the testing have said that they tested these bombs across the entire spectrum. Some of these tests happened underground but some were reportedly much closer to the surface, and the residents within a 300-mile radius of this island have all had varying degrees of reaction to this.

So even though there are many in the northern islands of the French Polynesian region who have been and continue to be all right, there are other, more concerned citizens who have begun asking questions and wondering aloud about the effects.

If you are still interested in finding out more about this place, then you should know that as a nonresident, people on French Polynesia are allowed to stay for three months without any kind of special permission. If you are bent on or otherwise obliged to stay over that three months, you need to apply for a long-term visa.

Isle of Man

Despite the fact that the Isle of Man is an island with associations with the United Kingdom, people from all over the globe have been flocking to this spot. For good reason—as one of the best tax options for the United Kingdom and Western Europeans, it is less than a half-hour flight from the mainland, making it accessible for everyone. Isle of Man offers a great deal to the person who is looking to move offshore to avoid tax payments and yet it also remains close enough so that the occasional visit is completely justifiable.

The principal drawback for people who are of French and German ancestry, and Western Europe, is that the main language spoken on this island is English. While much of the world is bilingual, those who are not could face challenges. However, if non-English-speaking individuals are able to keep their business off of the Isle of Man, they should be fine, and will not be assessed any taxes.

To see if you qualify for nonresident status, you should be able to pass this litmus test: 1) not a resident more than 182 days in any tax year, 2) not having stayed on the island for more than 91 days per tax year for four consecutive tax years, 3) you are a regular, nonaccidental visitor. While these may seem like somewhat stringent guidelines, the fact remains that even if you are a resident, you only pay low taxes.

On top of all that, you are on an island which is near enough for you to escape and get back to reality, yet you are removed enough to be able to just let all that noise wash off of you. The influence of Western Europe is apparent, but the Isle of Man is a creation all its own.

Madeira

If you are comfortable with your mobile income, living your mobile life style, and you have no need to make any money in the country, then Madeira may just be the spot for you. Quite popular with northwest Africans and southern

Europeans, Madeira offers tax-free living for six months out of the year, and if this suits you, then you should certainly move ahead with your plans.

If you have aims to open up a seasonal tourist business, make sure your operations last no longer than 120 days of the year. If your company or office operates just 120 days of the year on the island, then you are considered a resident. This is further complicated by the fact that Madeira is a Portuguese territory, so even if you only spend 120 days or less on this island, if you operate your business out of Portugal any other time of the year exceeding 120 days, then your business will be taxed at the Portuguese rate.

There are numerous benefits to the nonresident including tax-free living, so long as you are not earning any money from any Portuguese sources and so long as you do not overstay your 183-day welcome. Furthermore, if you overstay your welcome, then your world income will be taxed and you will need to report everything to the government. This includes employment income, commercial profits, capital gains, pensions, rental income, and a whole litany of the usual suspects. Corporate tax is moderate but if you are looking for a tax-fee existence, then you are better off not overstaying your 120-day corporate welcome.

Maldives

If you are a Muslim considering a big move away from Western society or if you are looking for something totally different as a place to set up a kind of resort, then the tiny island nation of Maldives may be just what you are looking for. Admittance as a resident is limited to convert Muslims and there is zero tolerance for any other faith. If you are not a Muslim, you may visit the island but any representation of any other deity will be confiscated before you are allowed from the airplane.

Furthermore, the practice of the residents of Maldives is to not allow non-Muslims citizenship. While this may not be a progressive way of thinking, it allows this nation to retain its identity and not be swayed from popular differing public opinion.

With a whole host of industries including fish processing, shipping, boatbuilding, coconut processing, woven mats, rope, handicrafts, coral mining, and tourism, the people of this tropical hot and humid area have a great deal of control over their tax burden. The personal tax burden is 0 percent. Personal tax is also 0 percent on nonresidents, although there are a number of import taxes which can vary widely depending upon the item which is being brought into the country. Furthermore, there is a 0 percent corporate tax on corporations.

However, people who feel they must fear the Muslim population should be aware that the people who live in Maldives are Sunni Muslim, if that means anything in particular to the individual. However, with a good communications setup in a stable social and political climate, the country of Maldives is the perfect place to set up some kind of an offshore resort for the nonresident or for the Muslim to go to and enjoy a tax-free existence.

Marshall Islands

While the world strives for order, harmony, and unity, there are some places which seem to be in existence for a certain task. You use the coffee machine for making coffee, shower head for taking a shower, and the dog brush for brushing the dog. In the spirit of that, the Marshall Islands is such a place. These islands are for incorporating both ships and corporations. That is it. There are no local attorneys, accountants, or other infrastructure. Often, people who are registering themselves as tax havens never actually visit the islands.

There are a number of reasons for this; among these is that two of these islands were former U.S. nuclear test sites, and one of the islands is still used as a missile testing range. But the other reason people often do not go there is that they do not have to.

With a full array of offices in New York, Zürich, Hong Kong, Tokyo, Rotterdam, and Piraeus, people are offered the ability to do all their business with these islands without ever leaving home.

If you do want to go visit these islands and you do want to stay on one of these islands, there is a 0 percent corporate tax for offshore businesses, a 0 percent personal tax for nonresidents, and a 30-day window where you can stay, with a 90-day extension possible. However, if you do spend more than the allotted first 30 days, they may ask you to take an AIDS test.

Mauritius

Grouped near the Seychelles, Mauritius is another island nation which may appeal to tax haven seekers. With an industry which includes such necessities as food processing, textiles, clothing, chemicals, metal products, transportation equipment, electrical machinery, and tourism, this tiny island boasts a great deal of an allure for the expatriate who is looking for a comfortable existence in a tax-free environment.

If you are looking for employment on the island, you should know there is income tax levied on these earnings; however, there are a great number of exemptions which are allowed should you be among the working class of the island. And while there are no withholding taxes on the island, the government is allowed to reach the same end by charging residents income tax and charging benefactors royalty payments. This ends up being a complicated equation, so you should be sure to speak to a tax professional that is familiar with this area before you take on Mauritius as your offshore tax haven.

A number of deductions are also permitted on the island and these include things like capital and investment allowances, interest costs, exchange losses from trading, reasonable renumeration for your directors, bad and irrevocable debts, approved pension contributions, royalties, trading losses, rent premiums, local taxes, and up to 200 percent of overseas marketing costs for your export or tourism business.

Though this may sound like a good deal on the surface, there are a number of deductions which are not permitted, including exchange losses on capital assets, excessive fees paid to directors, corporate income and capital gains, provisions, carried back losses, and other types of depreciation, so you should be sure to speak to a professional before you claim anything against this government, because you do not want to get run out.

There are a number of income taxes which are charged on the island; these include income from employment, allowances, bonuses, commissions, gratuities, pensions, annuities, dividends, interest, rent, and business income.

Believe it or not, there are a number of reasons to stay there, including the fact that as long as you do not stay more than 183 days in a tax year, you are granted nonresident status. However, you should know that the tax year ends on the 30th of June, so you cannot begin counting your days until the first of July and that will roll over into the next calendar year.

Mayotte

As another hedge-play, Mayotte, a small French island located in the Mozambique Channel, may be the jackpot for many people who are looking for an offshore tax haven. While it does have many positive aspects, Mayotte is a poor country with poor communications and not a whole lot of industry. They tried to make this island a tourist destination but that has failed. There are new industries available including a lobster and shrimp business which has revitalized the economy somewhat, but the hefty taxes on corporations located in the country make this a bit prohibitive.

With a 33.33 percent tax for businesses located in Mayotte and with few exemptions or other options allowed, many people who would be coming here for a tax-free life style may wish to not engage in any business practices. There is a 0 percent personal income tax on all money earned elsewhere outside of Mayotte, so for the person who has a mobile income or for the perpetually rich person based on their personal wealth or any stock plays they may have going on, Mayotte may be a place to consider.

However, the country is relatively undeveloped, 97 percent Muslim, has no banking system, and only one paved airport. If you are going to be operating your world business out of this country and the communications system is poor, you may wish to look elsewhere. Further complicating things is the fact that two thirds of the people here speak a Swahili dialect called Mahorian. So unless you are well schooled in Swahili or able to communicate in another manner, Mayotte may not be the place for you.

Mount Athos

Many people go after an offshore tax haven to save money and try to skate around the rules. However, there are some people who want to answer to a higher calling and for these people, perhaps Mount Athos is the way. As an area which is completely devoid of commerce and business and essentially all other types of communication, Mount Athos is a Greek Orthodox community which has over 2,000 residents who have devoted themselves to the monastic life style.

Mount Athos is one of the most beautiful places in all of Greece and asks for no taxes from any of its resident monks. If you are interested in going to visit this area, there are day trips which are allowed but you do need a permit. If you want to stay any longer — up to four days — there is a much more lengthy process involved. And if you want to be a monk and join these men on Mount Athos, then you need to be a Greek Orthodox to have permission. There are no women allowed by law.

While Mount Athos may not be the most progressive spot for an offshore tax haven, and while many people who may be reading this would wonder about people who would want to do this, there are people who have given themselves over to God or who see no other more noble calling in life, and for these people Mount Athos may just be the answer.

Nauru

As an island which is almost dedicated to offshore banking and the unofficial presence of companies, Nauru might just be a place for you. When planning your offshore tax haven, there are a number of things to consider; Nauru is a place with a 0 percent corporate tax and which has more registered offshore bankers than citizens who live there permanently. This makes it an ideal locale for a certain type of offshore tax haven seeker.

People who are looking for a little bit of a break on their

taxes can bet that Nauru is the place to be. While there are current economic and environmental challenges, the fact that the region is socially stable — and has a 0 percent tax rate for both businesses and 0 percent personal income tax — may be reason enough for you to look to this region for your business.

Currently, though, the livable situation is not ideal. With periodic droughts and rampant pollution due to the island's intensive phosphate mining business which has since declined, this is a place which needs to undergo a great deal of reinvention before becoming a place where most Westerners would be comfortable living.

New Caledonia

If you are able to juggle the needs of being a nonresident, not working, and shielding your income, then a place like New Caledonia may be an ideal one. However, if you are looking to stay for the long term and if you want to buy some property or if you want to form a company or if you plan on earning any amount of money while you are there, then you may wish to think of this as a vacation destination rather than as a full-time tax haven.

The reasons are threefold: one is the personal income tax. It goes up on a sliding scale from 5 to 40 percent depending upon how much money you make above $8,900. If you make less than $8,900, you are safe. However, the sliding scale goes up from there and it goes very sharply to 40 percent of your income above $40,050. So in a matter of $30,000, that is 40 percent of your income. That seems rather steep and it is. As a final note about your personal income: if you are a resident, taxes are not just on money you make while working on the island. The fact is that those 5 to 40 percent tax rates are on your world income, including property.

Another one of the big reasons you may not wish to seek solace at New Caledonia is because of the corporation tax. There is 0 percent corporate tax for nonresident companies. That is fine, but then you get into the situation of earned income, and if you are earning an income, you would hope that you are earning more than $9,000 on your corporation. If you are a resident, you get a 30 percent corporation tax flat out; there is also the trouble of a 35 percent corporation tax on mining companies.

Finally, the third reason you may wish to avoid this country is that it is a French territory inherent with all the entanglements which come with being a territory. All in all, though, this is a nice island to visit with a stable social economy and political makeup.

Niue

If you are reading this book and are at the beginning of your career domestically and thinking years and years down the road, then this may be a good page to earmark and check again much later. The fact is that Niue, which is a small island in the South Pacific, has faced numerous challenges in recent years. Although officially independent, Niue is most closely associated with New Zealand, and its economic well-being is in terrible shape.

Niue was a great place for offshore businesses and with that reputation unfortunately came the long arm of the law. Wherever good is being done there seems to be the following of corruption; the Organisation for Economic Co-operation and Development (OECD) is a partnership of many of the industrialized nations of the world. OECD strives to bring together governments of countries which are committed to democracy and the market economy; they tally the figures and level the playing field. However when the OECD found out about all the corruption going on in Niue, they pressured the government to shut down any offshore businesses.

There was much fraud and money laundering and who would have thought to look in this Oceanic nation were it not for the OECD? That said, it will be many years before Niue is fit to be called a good area to consider as am offshore tax haven.

There is also the much more practical fact that there are cyclones which are a persistent problem on this island and have caused many long-term investors to flee regardless. In 2004 there was a Force 5 level cyclone, the strongest level a cyclone can reach, which devastated the island and wrecked the country's infrastructure. This caused many of the residents of Niue to flee to the much more stable nation with which it is associated, New Zealand — and has left Niue virtually barren.

Norfolk Island

While many offshore tax havens have an advanced

system of government, paved roads, tall buildings, and ultramodern banking systems, that is often what people who are seeking offshore tax havens are looking to avoid. Take, for example, Norfolk Island. As a quiet location in the south Pacific Ocean near Australia, Norfolk Island is a perfect spot for somebody who is looking for that little bit of getaway. With a subtropical, mild climate and little temperature variation, the only thing to consider about Norfolk Island is the potential for typhoons. But people who are adventuresome are able to appreciate a place like Norfolk Island.

The island has a low gross domestic product and a poor system of communications, but that does not stop the people who live there from getting by with their day-to-day lives. They have a stable political and social climate and there is a 0 percent personal income tax for nonresidents. If you are deciding to leave the island there is a $25 departure tax. The corporate tax is also 0 percent for nonresidents and their tourist-related businesses may just be the niche for the right entrepreneur who is looking to capitalize on this and bring some attention to this tiny island.

If you are looking for the terms of your stay on Norfolk Island, there is a 30-day stay granted to nonresidents. Beyond that, you need to get an extension, which you may do for up to 120 days per year. However, many people choose to engross themselves in the life style, forget everything that they left back home, and end up becoming permanent residents altogether. And that is something that you could do as well.

Republic of Cape Verde

Another island nation which has a great deal to offer for people looking for an offshore tax haven is the Republic of Cape Verde. Its territory is a cluster of islands in the north Atlantic Ocean west of Senegal, and these Portuguese-speaking people are receptive to people looking to do business. With a whole host of local industry, including food and beverages, fish processing, salt mining, ship repair, and shoes and garments, the Republic of Cape Verde has many things going for itself.

However, just because it has things going for itself does not mean it would not be a good tax haven for you. In fact, it is a stable climate and offers great incentives for businesses and individuals looking to invest. With a climate that is both temperate and warm, the only things that the Republic of Cape Verde has going against it are naturally caused. Not only is it an island in the middle of the ocean which gets erratic rain, the Republic of Cape Verde suffers from a series of prolonged droughts and wind which can be very intense at times. There is also volcanic and seismic activity which exists below its surface, and, of course, the fact that it is in a politically and socially stable environment does not change the weather phenomena.

However, people looking to do business in this area of the world would be wise to consider the Republic of Cape Verde. Not only does it have all these other wonderful things going for it, but it also has many incentives for businesses and tax exemptions for investors who are looking to bring some commerce and some much-needed money to the area.

Samoa

Perhaps one of the sweetest deals in the south Pacific Ocean is the islands of Samoa. While residents may begrudge the steep tax rates of up to 39 percent on companies and up to 45 percent on personal income tax, if you are interested in taking your mobile business with you to the islands of Samoa you will pay 0 percent in taxes. You just need to be wary of the fact that you cannot carry on any of your business in Samoa with Samoans.

For investors, Samoa is a pretty good deal as well. The Samoans do not charge any capital gains taxes and dividend income is taxed at the top rate of 10 percent. If you are an offshore business person looking to establish a nonresident business, Samoa is not ideal because, while the 39 percent tax rate for resident businesses seems high, for nonresident businesses it is 45 percent.

With relatively good communications, tropical and rainy seasons as well as dry seasons, and the few tax-exempt offshore structures which should be investigated further, people looking for an offshore tax haven should consider Samoa.

Sao Tome and Principe

While this small island nation just off the West African shore may not be the spot for Westerners looking for a peaceful offshore tax haven, the economic growth and relative stability, compared with other West African nations, makes Sao Tome and Principe a positive spot for many who are interested in maintaining their West African identity and heritage but tired of the continued genocide.

In spite of the numerous changes in leadership as well as the coup attempts in 1995 and 2003, Sao Tome and Principe has a pretty decent track record. With steady economic growth and the recently discovered oil reserves off their coast, Sao Tome and Principe has taken positive strides toward becoming a strong leader in a number of important areas.

With many new projects pending and the preparation for further exploration, drilling, and cashing in on this new oil wealth, Sao Tome and Principe is poised to ascend to a new level of importance both in the region and across the economic spectrum. While not for the faint of heart, this may be an excellent investment opportunity for a wild-card play which could pay hefty dividends in the future considering the scarce supply and intense demand for oil resources.

Seychelles

There are a number of smaller nations which are found all over the world which present many great benefits to the person seeking an offshore tax haven existence. Many times these small nations will be under the umbrella of a much larger nation and such is the case for Seychelles. Located in the Indian Ocean and comprising many small islands which are spread out a great deal, the nation of Seychelles is part of the British commonwealth, yet it is also free from the tax burdens which exist in Great Britain.

With a tropical marine climate which is humid and lying just outside of the monsoon belt, Seychelles offers many of the benefits of tax haven status without a lot of the other utterances which make locating an offshore tax haven a problem. With official languages of English, French, and Creole, many Westerners would have a great deal of success living in this area. There is a 0 percent personal tax levied on people who are earning income from dividends and offshore work, and the mobile office is something which is welcome in a place like Seychelles.

If you have a job on this island, you will end up paying a small social security tax which has a varying rate, depending on the amount. However, if your job is just a supplement to your other offshore income or to your dividends from current holdings, you may not have to pay any tax at all.

Located in the British Indian Ocean Territory, an area known as the Chagos archipelago, the islands of Seychelles are just east of Africa and northeast of Madagascar. Despite the far-flung locale, this area of the world does remain under the rule of the Crown. You are also able to enjoy a nonresident status so long as you do not stay on the island more than 180 days in 12 months.

Singapore

A small island nation which is located just south of Malaysia and just north of Indonesia, Singapore is an excellent option for offshore tax haven status. Singapore should be considered by any mobile Westerner who is looking for a different place to relocate for their offshore tax haven. While Chinese, Malay, and Tamil are three of the official languages spoken in Singapore, English is also an official language.

Singapore is a developed nation with a flourishing consumer goods industry in things like electronics. There is also a bustling economy in chemicals, financial services, petroleum refining, oil drilling, rubber processing and products, processed food, ship repair, life sciences, offshore construction, and many other types of trade. There are nine paved airports on the small island nation and, unsurprisingly, they have an excellent communications system.

For businesses, there are a number of reasons to consider Singapore as an offshore tax haven. As a developing nation there is a rapid expansion in the country's assessment of taxes on things like capital gains, income, and sales of stock shares. However, the financial incentives in both the service and manufacturing industries are impressive. These include expansion and export incentives, deductions allowed for research and development, investment allowance incentives, overseas enterprises incentives, and development and expansion schemes meant to drive business, increase commerce, and raise this small, young nation's place to one where people want to put their money.

For the short-term expatriates who are interested in splitting their time with another location and are living solely off their capital gains, there is no capital gains tax assessed in the country of Singapore, with rare and particular exception. As long as you do not remain in the country more than 183 days in a year, you will be exempted from all tax on your Singapore-based income. There are also no gift taxes levied in Singapore and the estate duty is 5 percent for estates valued up to $5.7 million and 10 percent for any estates valued above that.

You should be aware that if you are a nonresident in Singapore and you take on work in the country, there are varying rates of income tax withheld. However, all foreign-source income earned while in the country of Singapore is untaxed.

St. Helena, Ascension, and Tristan Da Cunha

If you are looking for absolute seclusion and you want to get away from everything, then you may wish to consider this series of islands. While these are territories of the United Kingdom and English is the official language spoken on the island, these are some of the most remote islands in the world. With a population of less than 8,000 inhabitants and in the middle of the ocean between South America and Africa, you can bet that not many people are going to find you out there in the middle of nowhere.

With industries which include construction, crops, furniture, lacework, woodwork, and fishing, St. Helena and its outlying islands are the perfect escape for people who want to get away from everything. With a booming lobster business as well as other fishing industries going on in the area, St. Helena is a great place to escape for a little while. However, with active volcanoes in Tristan da Cunha and a GDP of $2500, St. Helena is not the place to be making any kind of money.

However, if you have a mobile business or if you have offshore investments and you are comfortable being so far away from everyone else, then maybe St. Helena is the perfect place for you. While you should not consider taking anyone there who is terminally ill or old, the young, virile, and adventuresome individual should be able to take on a place like St. Helena with a gusto and flair which may be inspiring.

St. Kitts and Nevis

Two small volcanic islands which are located in the eastern Caribbean, St. Kitts and Nevis are an excellent alternative for people who are interested in a tax-free life. Many people may feel constricted on an island like St. Kitts or Nevis; however, if you are looking for a completely removed existence and you are comfortable paying a little bit more for your goods and services, then this would appear to be a place for you to go. With a population of just around 40,000, these islands are small. And even though there are numerous beautiful beaches and plenty of relaxing, beautiful weather to be had, the truth is that they are isolated places so you should remember you are going to be away from everybody.

You would also need to get used to paying a lot more for everything. Just about everything needs to be imported, so there is a great deal of expense in just running what in the United States would be an ordinary life. You probably will have to be without a car; many people are not going to be comfortable with that, but that is just the way it is on these islands.

Both of these islands offer privacy protection, which is one of the great reasons to consider these islands as a possible offshore tax planning philosophy. There is no personal income tax but if you are thinking about forming a corporation, domestic companies face a tax rate of nearly 35 percent. While it is inexpensive to set up a company on the island, you should be aware of this before you do so. For people who work on the islands, there is also a social security tax of a paltry 5 percent against their monthly earnings which is capped off at $2,500 a month.

Investors will be pleased with the fact that there is no capital gains tax on either of these islands except when you sell local assets which you have owned for less than one year. Also, there is no EU savings tax directive, which makes a number of people satisfied with their choice to go to St. Kitts and Nevis over other nations in the Caribbean or the Channel Islands that are subject to EU taxes.

For a nonresident to invest in property, he or she needs to obtain what is known as an alien landholding license. You have to pay a duty fee and you should be prepared for a 10 percent markup to the price for these fees. The good news is that property is much less expensive than in other areas in the Caribbean, although the best properties still go in excess of $1 million.

To obtain a full-time residence permit, you have to complete a series of paperwork and you will need to prove or show the way in which you plan to make money while you are living on the islands. Evidence of assets and bank statements are helpful in the decision-making process, though they may order you and begin to ask for any other documents, so you should do a thorough investigation and find out what you are going to need before you show up empty-handed.

If you have the money to invest and you are interested in moving to St. Kitts and Nevis quickly, you can participate in a local investment program where you put back $250,000 into a local investment. This does come with some fees to the tune of tens of thousands of dollars for each family member, but you will be processed quickly.

St. Lucia

Another excellent spot for you to consider for your tax haven status is the island nation of St. Lucia. Cleverly situated within sight of the Caribbean, this is an ideal spot for people moving from locations in America, or people relocating from the high-tax area of West Indian origin. To become a resident of St. Lucia, you need to buy a property and to live there continuously for five years; you have the ability to become a full citizen after a period of seven years.

If you are not interested in becoming a citizen and just want to enjoy their income tax rate, there is a 0 percent corporate tax and a 0 percent personal tax. There are small stamp duties if you are acquiring property, but that is pretty much it. St. Lucia is subject to hurricanes and volcanic activity, which may make it somewhat problematic for some people. Their communications system is good and they have a direct association with the United Kingdom, so people looking for something a little more removed from society may wish to look elsewhere.

In terms of religious diversity, there is not a whole lot on this island as 90 percent or more of the religious affiliation on the island is Roman Catholic. English is their official language, which may make St. Lucia much more of a destination for Westerners than anyone else.

St. Martin/Sint Maarten

An island nation known as St. Martin/Sint Maarten is truly a thing all its own. With one side owing allegiance to France and one side being totally Dutch, this Caribbean island is an anomaly.

While moving here to live and work may not make a whole lot of sense, particularly if you are doing well for yourself— the highest-end tax rate is more than 57 percent — there are plenty of reasons for you to want to set up a business here. There are tax breaks which are afforded businesses as well as double-taxation treaties with countries like France and the Netherlands which may make doing your business here particularly smart.

However, in down markets a place like St. Martin could suffer a great deal. Not even due to the market pressure, but simply from the fact that its primary business is tourism, there are risks to forming your tax shelter and forming your business here. When money is not being made, people pull back and their money is not in the marketplace. The result is that the first business model which is hardest hit is tourism.

When tourism is not making any money then none of the locals are spending their money on your product, so unless you have a business plan that incorporates these people into your bottom line and gets them working for you to produce things or to ship things elsewhere, you may wish to consider another region of the world for your offshore tax haven.

St. Pierre and Miquelon

While many of these island nations that we are looking at are perfect in terms of weather and seem to be perpetually associated with tropical temperatures, there are some island nations that are not. St. Pierre and Miquelon is a cold and foggy area located approximately 800 miles northeast of Boston, Massachusetts and just south of Newfoundland.

From the name, you can imagine that St. Pierre is a French territory and operates under French law; although due to its proximity to the United States and Canada, there have been a number of adaptations which have made it more suited to its own area and its own needs.

St. Pierre and Miquelon seems to be stuck in its own mindset as it relies heavily on its main industry of fish processing and as a base for fishing fleets. The persistent fog makes travel into the area quite risky and dangerous if you like to go out on your boat. They have a fairly poor system of communications as many of the cellular and Internet companies have not yet reached that far north.

Also quite particular is the 99 percent Roman Catholic religious affiliation in the area. There is not a whole lot of variety in the area and with a fairly low GDP you could say that St. Pierre, despite all its tax benefits, could be not the best option for today's modern tax havens seeker.

St. Vincent and the Grenadines

Another beautiful Caribbean destination is St. Vincent. With a stable local government and a local crime rate which is low, you could say that St. Vincent is practically a perfect destination for the offshore tax haven seeker. Combine that with the official languages of English and French Patois, a good communications system, along with the fact that it is inexpensive to live there, and you have an excellent option for a tax haven.

The local government enjoys the site of an offshore tax seeker. They have a 0 percent personal income tax if you do not have local wages and you can even work there with a working permit as long as you are not competing for jobs with the locals. If you have your own mobile business, it is even better as the job will be practically transparent.

There is also a great deal of privacy and secrecy that goes along with St. Vincent. There is no reporting required for an international business corporation (IBC) and to get an offshore bank license is inexpensive. Considering that it is also only 1,500 miles from America, you are close if you ever need to get back home. There are six airports on the island; the only downside is there are no direct flights to the United States so you would need to transfer elsewhere within the Caribbean.

If you are interested in staying in St. Vincent as a nonresident, there are few restrictions. If you are interested in getting a permanent resident certificate, you have to invest $500,000 or more into a home on the islands. With a good mix of Anglican, Methodist, Roman Catholic, Hindu, Seventh-Day Adventist, and Protestant religions, there is a great deal of tolerance for just about everybody.

Tokelau Islands (Atafu, Nukunonu, and Fakaofo)

If you are the adventurous type who is feeling a bit bored with many of the more traditional offshore island tax havens, then perhaps you might wish to consider the Tokelau Islands. Located in the south Pacific Ocean and separated each by about 50 miles, these tropical, typhoon-prone, Polynesian outposts might just be what you are looking for. This secluded paradise is located in Oceania and is approximately halfway between Hawaii and New Zealand.

This is an island getaway destination which is truly "getting away." With a poor communications system, and the only access to these places being via ship, you could say that the Tokelau Islands are the last frontier in a manner of sorts. There is no tourism, no capital city, no banks, no harbor, and no airport. With few modern amenities, this is the perfect place for a hardened criminal or a lonely wayward soul to spend their days.

However, if you are looking to this as a move for your family or if this is going to be a permanent situation, you should know that the Tokelau Islands suffer from rising sea levels with their highest point being five meters above sea level. This is a contributing factor which could make it problematic to stay there for any period of time. If your interest lies in starting a corporation or if you have a group of people who want to try and relocate there, the lack of resources, high costs of import, and the inevitable high tax of insuring your venture could make it problematic. You might not get anyone to insure you on this island just due to its lawlessness and the lack of a social structure. If you combine that with the fact that the GDP on the island is a paltry $1,000, you would have a difficult time beginning an economy there, and it is not as if there is a whole lot of money to be spent and made there regardless. So as a permanent spot, the Tokelau Islands might not be a wise choice.

Tonga

There are some offshore tax havens which are all about the people and developing their own country. Many times, you will find an offshore tax haven which will have extreme benefits for people who are looking to come and stay and invest in the area. Tonga is one of these places. It has a low tax rate to begin with and you can all but eliminate any business taxes you may have by working directly with the government. The government offers all sorts of programs and tax exemptions on a long-term basis to foreign businesses that are looking to develop on the island.

While the communications system is poor in the south Pacific Ocean, on the island of Tonga there are a great deal of incentives for people looking to establish a business, perhaps in fishing — one of their primary industries — or tourism. If you are looking to open a small bed-and-breakfast, then you may be able to enjoy many of the tax breaks that the government is allowing for people who are bringing capital. While the corporate taxes which are on the books range from average to somewhat high, there are no taxes on things like payroll, local government, capital gains, probate, and export, and if you are able to work with the local government, then you may be able to avoid essentially all taxes.

If you are a nonresident looking at the island of Tonga as a place you may like to stay, you need to do it quickly because there is a 31-day visa period and that is it. After the first month you may be considered a nonresident and get taxed by not only the island of Tonga but also by your home country. When you get to the island of Tonga and you apply for your Visa, you need to show support for yourself for at least one month. You also need to have the money to buy your return ticket home before you will be granted any legitimate temporary resident status.

Trinidad and Tobago

One area in the Caribbean which is holding on to a different kind of old-world mentality is Trinidad and Tobago. Even though you are allowed to come and go from Trinidad and Tobago as you please, it seems to be that the only way to be able to enjoy their nonresident status is if you have relatives on the island. Staying with family is one of the oldest tricks in the book, but if you can invest money or if you have special skills that will benefit the island, they will also allow you nonresident status.

If you are looking to conduct any business in Trinidad and Tobago and you want to be a resident, it does not make much tax sense. There are free trade zones and offshore structures which even operate a 0 percent tax company, but there are also double-tax treaties with European countries and America that you need to be aware of. And if you rely on your relatives for your tax-free nonresident status, then you also need to make sure the family does not fall out of favor with any local high-ranking officials because then you could be run out on a rail regardless of what you do.

There is a fairly stable political and social climate in Trinidad and Tobago. English is the official language, although many do speak Hindi, French, Spanish, and Chinese, making it a well-rounded society in that regard. Also with Roman Catholic, Hindu, Anglican, Islam, and a large percentage of other religious tendencies for the residents of the island, you are bound to find something that suits your particular faith.

You need to be operating in a free trade zone as there is 0 percent personal tax if you are conducting your business offshore. However, if you are resident, then this tax can be levied up to 30 percent of your income. This is in addition to stamp duty and conveyance of real estate, real estate taxes, hotel room taxes, insurance premium taxes, road traffic license, vehicle transfer tax, gambling and lotteries, road improvement tax, and double-taxation treaties which exist and may raise or may lower your tax status.

In addition, the corporate taxes are fairly high at 20 percent withholding tax, royalties which are taxed at 20 percent, dividends which are taxed between 10 percent and 20 percent, and corporation tax which is 30 percent of profits. Petroleum companies are taxed at 35 percent, business levy is 2 percent, Green fund levy is .10 percent on gross sales and receipts, unemployment levy is at 5 percent, land operations at 5 percent, and marine operations at 55 percent, all of which make doing business on Trinidad and Tobago not much of a good idea.

This country is located in the Caribbean and with this comes advantages and disadvantages. Their stability in their political and social climate lies in their stepping up their claim against Venezuela, which is trying to invade the Caribbean in general. Many of the island nations have stood firm against Venezuela, and Trinidad and Tobago is one of those islands. In addition, they have a fairly good communications system, six airports, and an association with the United Kingdom which makes them strong in other regards.

As Trinidad and Tobago is in the Caribbean, you need to watch out for hurricanes and other tropical storms which could make your stay unpleasant.

Turks and Caicos Islands

A series of 45 islands which are located southeast of the Bahamas, the Turks and Caicos Islands has a total population of about 20,000 people and is a British territory, even though they enjoy self-rule under a governor and an elected council. The legal system on the Turks and Caicos Islands is essentially derived from English law, and English is the official language. Their economy is based primarily on financial services and tourism.

People who are looking to relocate to the Turks and Caicos Islands have plenty of reason to do so. There are miles of coral reefs and endless stretches of white sand beaches which are the perfect escape for any legal tax-evading citizen. Crime is pretty low in this area and they have a fairly modern telecommunications system and broadband Internet service. With direct flights to the United States and Canada, the Turks and Caicos Islands are a great choice for people who are interested in a tropical beach escape.

The Turks and Caicos Islands are quite similar to many of the other Caribbean islands in that there is no income tax, no capital gains tax, and no inheritance tax. The local government will generate money through indirect tax: import duties, stamp duties, and other such things.

Many people who are concerned about privacy would be pleased to know there is a strict banking confidentiality law which exists in the Turks and Caicos Islands which makes it a crime to allow unauthorized disclosure of confidential information. Tax matters are not included in any agreements that Turks and Caicos Islands have with the United States in terms of exchange of information.

If you are looking for property on the Turks and Caicos Islands, this can sway dramatically depending upon where you are looking. There are plots of land available for less than $50,000, or beachfront areas where you will pay more than $2 million. Some of the more basic apartments are available for around $250,000, but top-of-the-line condos are more than $5 million.

Due to the fact that everything needs to be imported, the cost of living can be high. If you want to make the Turks and Caicos Islands a permanent home, then you should consider obtaining a permanent resident certificate. You do this by making an investment in the local property or business. The minimum investment is $250,000 on the main island, Providenciales, and $125,000 on any of the other islands.

Once you have decided to become a permanent resident and you want to work, you need to obtain a work permit. If this is going to be a problem for you and you are going to need a job, do not go there right away, because many of the jobs which are available on the Turks and Caicos Islands are saved for locals. So unless you have a special skill, you may be put at the back of the line.

If you are interested in forming a business entity, you can do so without much difficulty. You can form an international business company, a limited partnership, a hybrid company, or a trust. There is no tax on any of these entities, and if you do form an international business company, you will receive a certificate of tax exemption for a period of 20 years, which guarantees you tax freedom for the next 20 years regardless of any other changes.

Tuvalu

People who are seeking an offshore tax haven are often seeking a respite from something else entirely. If you are looking for that little piece of heaven, and you feel like you need a break from just about everything in the modern world, you may wish to consider an island area that may be a little bit less developed. Tuvalu is one such place.

While many people may be afraid of a location where they cannot get their World Wide Web every day, others are seeking an escape from this drama, and the poor communication system in a place like Tuvalu allows you a respite from this — at least while their communication system remains poor. There is no visa requirement, but you are issued a visitor's permit when you arrive and you need to show that you have a flight elsewhere from there within the 30-day period.

As an area to live, there is not a whole lot of regulation going on in terms of personal income tax. There are sales taxes, however, which could make this area seem a little bit frenetic. The 40 percent tax on a nonresident company makes that option disagreeable; the 30 percent tax on resident companies is even par for the course. As a poor country with only one unpaved airport, you may think that a country like this would be unstable; nothing could be further from the truth. The people who live on his island are peaceful and the stability is a marked improvement from the "civilized world."

United States Virgin Islands

If you are a United States or Canadian citizen, the U.S. Virgin Islands may just be the perfect spot for you to enjoy your tax-free status. To be a nonresident on the U.S. Virgin Islands you need a visa and you cannot stay over 90 days. However, if you are Canadian or a United States citizen, you only need to prove your citizenship and you may stay indefinitely. There is a 0 percent income tax for nonresidents, so you would be a perpetual nonresident as a U.S. or Canadian citizen, paying 0 percent income tax.

The only caveat to your deciding to become a citizen of the U.S. Virgin Islands is that you would lose your right to vote in presidential elections.

With a stable political and social climate and an interesting mix of religious practices, starting with Baptist, Roman Catholic, Episcopalian, and other religious disciplines, the U.S. Virgin Islands seems to be a tolerant and peaceful place to live. There are natural disasters which could affect your decision to want to move to the U.S. Virgin Islands, including hurricanes, droughts, floods, as well as occasional earthquakes.

For corporations, moving to the U.S. Virgin Islands is a good deal as well. There are excellent communications to set up, no sales taxes, and 0 percent corporate taxes for exempt companies and foreign sales corporations. This means you need to apply for what is known as the Industrial Development Program and you will be exempt from all of your taxes and pay a small 1 percent customs duty. If you are not exempt from these taxes, there is a graduated rate with a ceiling of 38.5 percent, a small real estate tax, a fairly small gross receipts tax, and a small customs and excise tax; all of which could make that exemption even that much more important.

If you are independently wealthy and interested in finding a great place to stay near the United States, you may wish to consider the U.S. Virgin Islands. With a good mix of English, Spanish, and Creole as well as their own use of the U.S. dollar as their form of currency, the U.S. Virgin Islands could be the perfect spot to settle down for the United States expatriate.

Vanuatu

Another place to go if you are looking to get away from everything is Vanuatu. This beautiful but remote place which is located in the South Pacific is a fairly simple place to live and has some governance by the United Kingdom and France. It is a series of islands located in the South Pacific that charges 0 percent personal income tax so long as the business conducted is not done locally.

With 30 airports connecting all of these islands and the official languages of English, French, and Pidgin all fairly well understood on the island — despite their 100 local dialects — this is a tropical paradise for somebody looking to get away from everything and just chill out. With a colorful mix of Presbyterian, Anglican, Roman Catholic, Seventh-Day Adventist, Church of Christ, as well as other indigenous beliefs and even a few cult members on these islands, the people here all get along surprisingly well and it is relatively peaceful. Also surprising to many is the fairly comprehensive communication system including cellular, land line, and Internet connections.

Even if you are considering conducting business on this island, the domestic taxes are fairly well kept in check. You will be subjected to some import and business license fees, but if you are from Australia, Fiji, Japan, Hawaii, New Zealand, or any other South Pacific or Oceania area, this is the ideal tax haven for you.

Wallis and Futuna Islands

It appears that all the major players on the world stage have a claim somewhere in the south Pacific Ocean and France is no different. France has a cluster of islands known as the Wallis and Futuna Islands. These islands experience weather much the same as other islands in the south Pacific Ocean, with tropical hot and rainy seasons and cool dry seasons as well as typhoons and other extreme weather conditions.

While you may be fooled by neighboring Polynesian islands, the truth about these pair of island groups is that they are subjected to excessively high rates of unemployment. With an entire populous — near 90 percent — who are continuously or intermittently out of work and thus continuously or intermittently live their lives subsidized by the government, how could any intelligent business person expect to make any money?

For this reason, it does not make a whole lot of sense to be doing business someplace where there is not any money to be made. If you have some plan to get the economy rolling again and you feel like you could make money off of your own wages that you are paying out, then that might be one thing. However, you should approach any business ventures in this area of the world with caution because you do not want to be stuck with worthless property that you cannot sell or even give away to anyone.

Focus on Europe

Many people who are fed up with the United States' role in government in general and taxes specifically may be wishing to change their lives completely and upend themselves to another corner of the globe. An island nation or some remote, unsettled territory with little government oversight and complete self-reliance may be just up the alley of the Libertarian in your sphere.

However, even though in idealistic terms this may sound just peachy, there is potential peril fraught with that. You could fall on tough times or your employer could fire you. Even if you are self-employed, your business model could become outdated. If you are relying on return from investments and you are not linked up to Berkshire Hathaway or Google stock, there is no guarantee. Even having a giant with a prominent place in your portfolio, or with a well-diversified mix, stranger things have happened. This is a challenge to every investor, and especially if you have or one day aspire toward a spouse and children, there is implicit risk in that life style that many are not prepared for.

While many people reading this book may be beyond that stage in their life, for the elderly, there is an entirely different set of challenges which need be faced. If you have spent your whole life living and working in a country where there are taxes and social security, you may feel as though you have already paid in too much and have too much of a vested interest in remaining. Even if you feel that your taxes are too high and that you have many more good working years remaining, many will wonder why they would consider leaving and would dread what may happen to them should some calamity befall them in an ungoverned place.

So many would choose to be close to something familiar—some mix of low tax, no tax, yet with many of the bureaucracies Americans are used to, like the post office, police, hospital, firefighters, McDonald's, and Starbucks easily at your disposal. While all of these things are found in most civilized nations in the world, it is in the prevalence of these things where many of us make our judgments.

To alleviate this fear, many Americans looking to break free from the strains of the Internal Revenue Service will escape to a European nation. For the purpose of discussion, we are dealing only with places within the European continent. Most of these countries are places that Americans are familiar with, at least in theory. More likely though, some of these seemingly familiar places are foreign indeed, regardless of what you think you know, so you should fully investigate the country, region, and locality that you are considering for your tax refuge.

Although they are some of the strongest allies of the United States, there are pitfalls in many English-speaking EU nations which need to be taken into account. However, there are places within the EU that can be excellent alternatives to the U.S. if you are looking to permanently relocate.

Andorra

One of the best tax havens in all of Europe is a country you may not even be familiar with. Perhaps you do not even remember this country when you were listing off the countries of Europe from memory for your geography class in middle school. Andorra might not have even been recognized by some geography teachers just because it seems so inconsequential. At just over 180 square miles and with one main road connecting it from Spain on one side to France on the other side, Andorra is very small indeed. By that reasoning one may even regard this place as a sort of forgotten country.

But not for the person who is looking for a tax haven country. Andorra is a true tax haven paradise. With a state which has no income tax, no capital gains tax, no gift tax, no inheritance tax, and no capital transfer tax, Andorra is something of a self-sufficient country, as it makes all of its money from itself. Tourism brings 80 percent of the GDP of Andorra. And while virtually none of its land is able to be farmed, the country relies heavily on its tourism destination as it the off-the-beaten-path midpoint between Spain and France.

Another big draw to the area of Andorra could be the fact that the people who live there seem to be doing something right. Residents of this tiny enclave are said to have the longest life expectancy of any country in the world; this could be because of its climate and geography. There is a lot of sunshine, the area is surprisingly dry, and its perch inside the mountains is a great spot for older people who experience tightness in the chest and have trouble breathing. Andorra is also a great destination for people with chronic asthma symptoms or a lifelong battle with the disease. Long life may not be important to some younger swingers and it may be tougher to stage a Broadway show or run for office, but the facts remain that we are only as much as the sum of all of our parts; for this reason it should be remembered that Andorra may be a great place to live.

The two closest airports are three and a half hours away, so you need to drive a bit of a way to get to Andorra; but once there, many people never want to leave. Property prices have been on the rise in Andorra for some time, but they are still reasonable by many estimates. This is probably because of its relative difficulty to get to and its single entrance and exit point off the main thoroughfare.

Outside of the difficulty to get there, perhaps the biggest detriment against Andorra as a tax haven is the restrictions they have on allowing people to live there. If you are looking to get a tourist visa, it is usually acquired without much difficulty. But if you are looking for a longer-term stay, you need to have either a work permit or a passive residence permit. Work permits are not given to self-employed foreigners and are only issued to people who were working for an Andorran person or an Andorran company. Typically these go out to European Union nationals first and only if there is no Andorran who is qualified to do the job. Therefore, most people who are coming to Andorra to escape the tax burdens need to be able to live off their own investments and obtain a passive residence permit.

Getting these passive permits will remind any American of the bureaucratic mess of getting anything done in the United States. For this reason, if you are unfamiliar with the task at hand, you should definitely see about employing the wisdom of somebody who is an Andorran who can help walk you through the process. Residence will be granted for one year and renewals are for every three years following that. One of the things you need to do to get this passive residence permit is a signed statement saying you will live in Andorra for least six months every year. Their manner of assurance of this is, at the time of renewal, you must bring your utility bills for close inspection.

Another thing every person needs to do is deposit $30,000 with the government per couple. You do not get any interest on this money, so this could be something of a turnoff to many people who do not appreciate passive money; however, if you want to see about getting a place in Andorra and you are interested in finding out more, you should do that. Another thing you need to be able to prove is an income of more than three times the average wage in Andorra when you move there. Health insurance is also required, and you need to be able to prove that you own or are able to rent a house in Andorra before you will be approved. The $30,000 deposit is returned in full when you leave.

Most of the people who live in Andorra have been there for some time, so there is not a big influx of rebel people from all over the world coming into Andorra. With that in mind, if you only speak English your options for conversation and entertainment are limited.

Campione

Heralded as the best place to live for individuals who have a high net worth, Campione is an Italian town that offers all the benefits of living in Switzerland without any of the tax burden. Although the cost of living is high, the benefits are multiple for people who live there. You have no VAT, no personal income tax on income earned outside of Italy, no municipal taxes, and all profits from bank deposits, shares, bonds, real estate, and other transactions from a Swiss or international stores are never registered for tax purposes for residents of Campione.

With a stable political and social climate as well as just one road leading into and out of this area and no restrictions on nonresident stay, this is a wealthy person's tax-free dream. Because of the fact that there are no banks anywhere in this city, you do need to go to Switzerland to do your banking, but for the people who live here, that is not a problem.

Campione is located in what is known as the Swiss Canton Ticino, which is a ten-minute drive from Luano and 45 minutes on the highway from Milan. Campione is an Italian enclave which is located in Swiss national and economic territory as it is completely surrounded by Switzerland. There are no border controls, though, so you can pass into and out of this area with freedom.

Even though all of the social services — post office, telephone, traffic laws, and car license plates — bear Swiss burden, there is none of the tax burden. Furthermore, unlike Switzerland, there is no problem for foreigners with money to spend looking to establish residence there. All you need to do is have a house or apartment in Campione and you will be granted a residence permit.

Even though residents are free from Swiss law, they are subjected to the Italian tax law because Campione is a territory of Italy. Still, there are special requirements for Campione residents. Among these is that there is no personal income tax, no municipal tax, and residents are not subject to the double-taxation agreements of Switzerland that are shared with Canada, the United States, and most of Western Europe.

Another benefit is that companies in Campione have some advantages over Swiss companies. They are able to carry what appears to be a Swiss address, use Swiss banking facilities, and still are not subjected to Switzerland's high income and withholding taxes. All an interested individual needs to start a company in Campione is around $1,000, the same as in Italy, and while it may take a little longer than in Switzerland, you have those beautiful Swiss Alps to look at and enjoy every day.

Denmark

It should be no surprise that a country as old as Denmark

has some archaic laws when it comes to their tax system. And anybody who is familiar with Hamlet knows how the Prince of Denmark settles scores against people who owe him. So if you are looking for a personal offshore tax haven, Denmark may not be the place for you.

However, Denmark is an acceptable place to set up a holding company if that is something that you are looking to do. However, with all the other hurdles and challenges in front of you, you may wish to consider having your holding company set up elsewhere. The only caveat to that could be if personal matters brought you to the country often or if you have contacts back in Denmark who could act on your behalf.

If you are looking to move to Denmark permanently, that is something else entirely. It requires a great deal of paperwork and jumping through hoops which may be cumbersome to many. You need to have specialized education or a skill which is in limited quantity within the country. While the world is getting more and more specialized and people are becoming experts for just about everything, if you feel you can market yourself as valuable to the nation there is the one great benefit of a pretty solid social security package which will be bestowed upon you on retirement.

However, if you have great skills or these other traits you could probably make use of them much better in another country and just go and visit Denmark in your free time.

France

Paris is one of the most cosmopolitan, romanticized cities in the world. Who does not know the images of the Eiffel Tower? Who has not seen the windswept, cobblestone streets with two beautiful, thin people smoking hand-rolled cigarettes, sipping cappuccino, and not looking at one another?

While all of these images are interesting and some may exist in our subconscious, the truth is that France is not these images of Paris. It is an industrious world superpower with more than two and a half million private enterprises in this relatively moderate-sized country.

Even despite its smallish size, France is home to the fifth largest economy in the world; it is the fifth largest exporter and fourth largest importer of manufactured goods. For all the grief the people from Paris get in our subconscious, France is certainly a vibrant and lively economy. Another interesting fact about France is that this nation is an extremely ethnically diverse one. With an estimated 4.9 million foreign-born immigrants, France is the leading asylum destination in Western Europe. So even without a dicey offshore tax haven status, it is a great place for people to migrate to when they have tired of their home nation.

You should be careful to learn the language, though. Even though many French nationals are multilingual, there is an article in the French constitution, Article 2, which states that French is the sole official language spoken in France.

This makes the country the only Western nation to have only one officially recognized language.

The only situation in which France is a good offshore tax haven is if you are a holder in a large multinational corporation or if you operate a business; they will give you special tax concessions for relocating offshore. People who want to go to France and spend their days there are typically advised to go for their 183 days and then leave before that time is up. The tax repercussions on the other side are way too hefty for anybody who is looking to save any money to justify it.

Going right along with that argument is the fact that you should never buy a villa unless you are able to remove yourself from ownership of it through an offshore trust of some kind. France has not made a great fuss over people who are avoiding their taxes in the past, but that dynamic is shifting slowly and France is beginning to wake up to the fact that they are missing out in tens of millions of dollars in unpaid tax revenues and the future could be bleak for people who come to France to escape the tax man.

Ways to be deemed a tax resident are not only if you stay over the 183 days or if you have a home in France, but also if France is a place of your principal residence, France is the place you perform your principal professional activities, or France is a center of your economic interests. You should certainly look into this with your tax consultant if you are concerned at all that you could be owing taxes to the French government because they could certainly come after you.

Germany

As a large and active country in not only the European Union but also in the world political stage, Germany has many taxes it levies to keep its economy and government running. Although there are certain stipulations within the German economy which will allow for somebody seeking an offshore tax shelter to take respite there for their six months out of the year as well, there are provisions and reductions which are allowed in certain circumstances.

If you are interested in investing in Germany in any kind of a legitimate way, you can work out different particulars with your tax advisor. In general, there are certain real estate capital gains rollover tax reliefs which are allowed and there are even grants available if you are a manufacturer in Germany and you plan on keeping your manufacturing plant in Germany for a period of time.

Another place where businesses are able to benefit from the tax relief is in the corporate tax rate which is allowed to be adjusted depending upon certain stipulations. Also, Germany is flexible on taxation when it comes to trade tax. Furthermore, income tax from capital investments are often granted tax breaks.

Tax breaks are well deserved in this area due to the fact that the VAT in Germany is a hefty 16 percent. If you are importing or exporting food or printed material, your rate is just 7 percent, which is reasonable.

If you are a religious person and you are interested in becoming associated with one of the churches in Germany there is also a church tax of between 8 percent or 9 percent. However, if you do not need to be officially affiliated with the church, you do not need to pay this tax.

Single taxpayers are granted some relief so long as their income is below $7,664 for single taxpayers or $15,328 for married taxpayers.

While the limit on a stay in Germany is 183 days within any 12-month period, you should know that renting a property or doing any kind of business in Germany for more than three months at a stretch will also make you subject to taxes on not only your German income but also your worldwide income and your assets.

Greece

With one of the oldest civilizations known to man and with a 98 percent religious populace, the country of Greece has gone through numerous changes in its long and storied history. However, this may not be the place for you to take tax-sheltered residency unless you have some aim to stay there and do business there. Greeks are proud of their culture, heritage, and their tradition and 99 percent of the population speaks the official language of Greek. If you are not willing to pay this area of the world some lip service in some respect than you may do better elsewhere.

For the person who is curious and interested in learning about things and is quick at picking up customs and traditions, or for the person who is brought up Greek in another country, returning to Greece to do your business is a great thing. With its main industries of food and tobacco processing, textiles, chemicals, metal products, tourism, petroleum, and mining, the Greeks have a number of popular incentives to bring people from far and wide. In fact, the Greek market encourages foreign investments and this is something which should be remembered when you are considering Greece as your offshore tax haven.

However, if you stay more than 183 days in a year you will be required to pay taxes from 5 percent up to 40 percent of your world income, so nothing is off limits to the Greeks. You may be better off living in a nearby country and just doing business in Greece if that is your intent. If you are planning on being an employer and employing people, you need to contribute 20 percent of their salary to social security. This seems like a big contribution and it is, but as long as you are able to keep your income out of the country, then you could end up prospering a great deal for your time in Greece.

Iceland

While Iceland is an island nation, it should be included here in the section on Europe and the United Kingdom because of its standing as a large European nation. Iceland is one of the better deals you can get in Europe and is attractive to foreign corporations.

The 18 percent corporation tax on net income in Iceland is pretty fair; however, its lack of taxes on received dividends makes it that much more of an attractive option. If you are talking about profits from different branches of your business, then those are tax exempt, and when there is no double-tax treaty, Iceland will offer foreign tax credits to aid in double taxation.

There is also no VAT on exported goods and services from Iceland, making it that much more of an attractive place for you to set up your business in Europe. While the temperature may freeze many people out, Iceland is one of the better options for this area of the world when it comes to offshore tax havens.

With a stable political and social climate and a number of industries, as well as fishing and tourism and a fairly large GDP by comparison to other attractive tax havens, Iceland is definitely a location you should consider when you are scouting out your offshore tax haven.

Ireland

Many people like to escape their native country when they are sick of the city life. For this reason, some people end up going to a place like Ireland. Going to Ireland is a great idea if you are looking to stay as a nonresident for less than half of the year. If you stay for more than six months in any one year or more than 240 days over any two consecutive years, then you will be taxed as a resident. Ireland's personal taxes are quite high and can reach as much as 44 percent on some income, so you should plan accordingly.

Ireland is a great place to go for entrepreneurs if you are

looking for low labor costs, a 20-year tax holiday, and free government money to fund your startup costs for your new business. Ireland is the only European Union country which offers entrepreneurs benefits of an English-speaking workforce, labor costs that are 60 percent below U.S. levels, and a 10 percent ceiling on taxes. Since the 1970s, the Irish government has been pursuing an aggressive foreign investment program to encourage entrepreneurs to set up shop in Ireland.

Evidence of this is the Irish Development Authority (IDA), a government-controlled entity which is looking to generate foreign investment capital. The IDA also has broad powers to approve applications and make grants to prospective employers. With branch offices in the United States, Australia, Japan, South Korea, Taiwan, Great Britain, Germany, and the Netherlands, the IDA is an aggressive vehicle indeed.

While foreign investors may be hesitant to move abroad and set up a business, there are grants allotted for the creation of jobs, and all that a potential business person needs to do is go to their local offices in their home country. This allows many business persons to cut through the red tape which is typical of foreign investment in foreign countries and get right to the business of doing business which is what everybody wants. And big or small, Ireland is looking for your business.

Businesses which are looked upon most favorably include manufacturing or international services. International services are a broad palette which includes computer or software services, bank offices for insurance companies, and financial or other assistance.

If you are trying to decide whether or not to go to Ireland to start your business, you should be aware that Ireland and the IDA look favorably upon businesses that will employ many of Ireland's university graduates — to keep the smart kids local and contributing to the local economy. Not surprisingly, with all of the local support and all of the businesses who have landed and been successful in Ireland, many smaller companies have grown to become medium- and larger-size companies in their first few years in the country.

There is also a program known as the Shannon Free Zone. This adds incentives which are similar to those offered by the IDA for companies that are located near Shannon Airport.

Many of the top names in the world have opened up European hub offices in Dublin's International Financial Services Center (IFSC). These include such businesses as IBM, Alcan, Volkswagen, Volvo, Grand Metroplitan, and Outokumpu. Other familiar business names like Asea Brown Boveri (ABB), BMW, Ericsson, and Coca-Cola have made the IFSC the hub by which they manage their worldwide insurance needs.

The IFSC has proven to be one of the most successful business rejuvenation ventures in the world. With more than 195 products approved and commitment to employ 3,000 people, the IFSC has helped transform the once-derelict dock area of Dublin into a thriving European financial center.

Ireland exists outside the framework of a more established territory because it is in rapid flux and constant development. By that rationale, you should certainly check up on what is going on in Ireland at this moment to try and see if any of this will fit your individual situation. You can certainly take advantage of many of the offshore tax benefits of a rapidly changing, expanding, growing, and cultivated environment as long as you are able to show the area why they need your individual enterprise or person in this space rather than someone else.

There are still benefits for the individual as well. There are personal allowances which are granted in numerous situations, including for couples or if you have mortgage interest pension contributions or any number of other things. However, you do not want to stay more than six months in any year if avoiding taxes is what you are after. While the green country in Ireland is a beautiful thing to see — and you should make sure to kiss the Blarney Stone while you are there — personal tax avoidance is a slippery slope to navigate in Ireland.

Jersey

This is one of the island nations which could have been included in the island section, but due to its close-knit affiliations with France and the United Kingdom, Jersey has earned its spot here. Located in the English Channel with excellent communication systems, the island of Jersey is a place where many French- and English-speaking individuals end up escaping to.

Essentially you can live here for free. As long as you do not do any business or earn a wage on this island, you can literally live there for nothing. There is always nice weather in Jersey and with a relatively easygoing life style, many people could not ask for much more.

Companies on the island of Jersey are treated as individuals so the same rules apply. If you own a company on this island it will be taxed at 30 percent. Furthermore, if you are a nonresident living on Jersey and you have a trust, this often will seek the ire of the tax man.

However, as long as you collect all your money in the beginning of the year and you do not stay there any more than 182 days in any tax year, you will be safe. You may begin to be seen as a resident if you stay there 91 days per year for four consecutive tax years. Or if you visit regularly and your visa visits are not an accident or due to some particular occasion, they could also consider you a resident and charge you the tax which a resident would pay. However, even if you are a resident, you will only pay VAT and no tax on your onshore interests. If you work or own a business, you will end up paying the appropriate income and social services taxes.

Liechtenstein

Another favorable locale for the world traveler is the

country of Liechtenstein. Fully landlocked and small, the 34,000 people living there all share a common thread in that they are able to enjoy the relieved burden of a low tax existence. There is still a tax on income derived from work for all residents; you are considered a resident if you have your permanent residence on property within the country's borders or if you live in the country and either work or own a business in Liechtenstein.

One of the biggest things to concern yourself with about Liechtenstein is being caught for not playing by the rules. That is, the officials in this tiny area are suspicious of people who go to their country for any reason; therefore, they are expecting you to be there for tax avoidance and your paperwork will be highly scrutinized. When you are first getting set up inside the country, it is a good idea to use an entity inside the country to alleviate any suspicion and make sure you do everything you are supposed to.

Another thing that should be made note of about Liechtenstein is that it is a civil-law country, not a common-law country. It owes a great deal of its legal heritage to Swiss and German ancestry. By that rationale, any well-studied individual in tax avoidance would expect trusts and trust-like institutions not to be possible. Much to the joy of the interested individual, though, they are.

Despite the fact that it is a landlocked country, Liechtenstein is not a geographically isolated country. It is located just between Austria and Switzerland off the banks of the Rhine River, is 16 miles long, and averages 3.7 miles in width. Though there are no airports in the country, one of the easiest ways to get to Liechtenstein is to fly to Zürich and drive from there or fly to any other European capital and take the train.

For all intents, though, you should be able to avoid many of the traps if you are a transient resident. One of the benefits to incorporating your company there would be security, protection, and secrecy. In addition, you would be granted a low tax burden which would make this a great stopover from its neighboring states of Austria and Switzerland where taxes are a little bit out of control.

There are legal codes which originated in the Austro-Hungarian law. Local legislation was enacted in 1914 and was influenced by both the German legal tradition and Swiss property law. In 1926 there was a locally originated code dealing with property which is advantageous to the tax haven seeker. What the tax code says is that basically a holding company is exempt from capital and earnings taxes.

A holding company is one that owns part or all of other companies' outstanding stock. The holding company is typically one which does not produce goods or services itself; its only purpose is owning shares of other companies. This allows for the reduction of risk for the owners and a hand in many different types of industries. By this reasoning, a company such as this will pay minimal annual tax on its total paid-up capital and reserve capital.

Liechtenstein also allows an even better tax deal to "foundations," which are completely unique and local creations. Foundations not only enjoy a special sliding tax rate on capital, but they are also exempt from the registration requirement in the commercial register — so they have the advantage of privacy along with that of virtually no tax. Family foundations and ordinary foundations are the two types of tax structure and family foundations are granted the benefits on all capital over 10 million Swiss francs where ordinary foundations need to achieve only 2 million Swiss francs to participate in the sliding scale.

Secrecy is also an important component to the Liechtenstein tax advantage. With a more true preservation of the Swiss banking tradition than Switzerland and with no international commitment to relax their secrecy laws, Liechtenstein is one of the best places to go if you are looking for paramount secrecy.

In addition, there are unique legal entities inside of Liechtenstein: the foundation and the establishment. The foundation is only slightly different from a trust. Foundations are set up to allocate future property to family members or other beneficiaries and are created with an original endowment. Rather than there being a trustee, there is a board who manages the principal fund and makes grants to the intended beneficiaries out of returns on investment, principal invested, or both.

But a foundation does not need to be limited to these narrow functions. Foundations are able to manage one's estate with the benefit of taxable returns derived by a separate legal entity. Foundations are not taxed locally if their principal involvement is investment in other companies or if they have no local business involvement apart from their own management. Foundations are also able to be handled in a private manner separate from the state because no state registration is required.

An establishment is something else that a tax haven seeker in Liechtenstein may wish to consider. The establishment will have a founder and the founder is a legal personality, not necessarily an actual person. The only requirements of an establishment are that the founder has his or her name on the certificate and the founder must sign the articles of incorporation and the signature must be notarized.

There are a few things that the articles of the establishment must specify: name of the establishment, purpose of the establishment, capitalization, organization, methods of accounting, and provisions for liquidation. an establishment also must be registered by the state and if it does business locally it must pay capital tax plus a profits tax.

If you are considering setting up an establishment in Liechtenstein, there are a few generalities. Annual figures will vary widely. Whether or not an establishment makes sense for you here depends upon your individual circumstances and what you are setting out to accomplish.

However, with an excellent communication system, a fairly high GDP, and a number of industries which are all cutting edge, including electronics, pharmaceuticals, precision instruments, and other things, Liechtenstein may be a perfect spot for you if you are looking to get away from it all right in the middle of Europe. And with all of the benefits of Swiss-type bank facilities and monetary freedom and absolute privacy, Liechtenstein may just be the perfect place for you to go to set up your offshore tax haven.

Livigno

As a mostly cold and dry Alpine region in northern Italy, Livigno is a 0 percent tax haven. For the skier in all of us, this is a perfect setup, as you have little interruption from tourists due to the fact that in the winter this place is not accessible except through a three-mile tunnel starting in Switzerland.

However, this is a little bit of a blessing and a curse. Livigno is a fantastic place to live, particularly if you are Italian or if you are Swiss, and the 0 percent personal tax makes it the perfect place for you to set up shop if you are interested in a life spent in the mountains.

It is near the airports at Milan and Zürich, and even though it is accessible only by road and rail, this is a town which thrives off tourism from ski resorts and other related industries such as restaurants and hotels. It is probably these seasonal guests who have helped put a place like Livigno on the map, so to speak.

This is an economy which is booming and will continue to as long as there is expendable income for people to go skiing. So if you are interested in opening up a tiny bed-and-breakfast in a mountain town, and if you have a good lead on some property that is coming available, you should go for it. If you are a recent retiree or if you are interested in skiing for yourself, then a place like Livigno may just be the perfect spot for you.

Luxembourg

While this beautiful country may not be one for you to live in just due to its high taxes on net worth and assets, Luxembourg may be the perfect place for you if you are interested in setting up an offshore business structure through any one of its numerous formulas. Incorporating inside of Luxembourg is easy as long as you have an offshore advisor who would be able to help you utilize the structure to your best advantage. In fact, you may be able to cut your withholding and your income taxes to the bare minimum through any one of their structures.

Luxembourg has a number of different strategies set up for people looking to invest as they see fit. You can set up a joint stock company, limited liability company, general partnership, limited partnership, overseas company, or holding company for your different businesses.

Luxembourg is also becoming the place where U.S. mutual funds invest. There are also a number of benefits to such things as financial service companies, insurance companies, and ship management and maritime operations. Believe it or not, if you run a ship management or maritime operation company from Luxembourg, you will receive many favorable tax advantages. This is sort of misleading as Luxembourg is fully landlocked on either side of Belgium, Germany, and

France. Many people shy away from Luxembourg due to its corporate taxes, which are high — up to 47.15 percent.

Luxembourg is a favorable place to set up your holding company for a number of other reasons. None of your books will ever be examined or supervised by any authority. In addition, their liberal judicial system tends to go the way of the holding company. Regardless of your profits, there is a small annual tax and there is no communal taxation, making it a great find in the offshore tax haven arena.

Furthermore, none of the principals of your holding company need to live in Luxembourg. This means your promoters, directors, auditors, managers, and anyone else can all be of foreign nationality and can live elsewhere, where personal taxes are lower. Also relating to holding companies is the fact that there is no tax levied on dividends or foreign securities which are held by the company. Additionally, the law does not require that any list of your holding company's securities be released at any time. With their lax judicial system and these laws and precedents in place, you can plant your money and watch it grow.

Even though this country has double-taxation agreements with countries such as Holland, France, Austria, the United States, and the United Kingdom, this should not discourage you from forming your holding company. The simple reason is that Luxembourg holding companies are not taxed in the first place. You are able to avoid these traps and coast to a cool, easy ride while you are here.

Finally, Luxembourg is a nice place to stay. However, if you are looking for a permanent locale, you may wish to reconsider. As a temporary place to stay Luxembourg will allow you six months until tax will be levied against your worldwide income. Just be sure to get out before the six months are up and you should be fine; however, the taxes due range from 13 percent to over 47 percent on your personal income. That is a large amount which could turn your whole perspective on this fine European nation sour in a hurry.

Monaco

Many people are familiar with the image of Monaco and Monte Carlo as places of disrepute and excess, where crime, prostitution, and other morally questionable activities take place. However, Monaco may be so much more than that for the seeker of an offshore tax haven. If you are not an employer or employee, Monaco may just be the place for you to whittle away the rest of your days. There are a number of ways in which you can avoid paying taxes in this peninsula and they all involve being independently wealthy. Essentially, you just need to not do any business or employ anybody in Monaco.

With a number of manufacturing-type jobs which go on in Monaco, it should be no surprise that nonresident tax status within the community is not held in high regard. However, with a 0 percent personal income tax, Monaco may just be the place for you to go.

With an over 95 percent Roman Catholic populace, there

is a definite predominance in terms of religion. So much so, in fact, that there are no mosques or synagogues anywhere in this principality. If you are a non-Christian or a non-Catholic and you need a place to worship, the area of Monaco may not be the place for you.

The Netherlands

If you are looking for a place to stay where you can enjoy yourself for as long as you like, then the Netherlands may just be it. The Netherlands is where you will be able to stay indefinitely, as your world income is not taxed. However, you cannot work in the Netherlands or run a business from there. There are a number of ways in which you can make your business completely profitable through a Dutch holding company. But this becomes complicated when you are talking about dealing with Holland and the Dutch Antilles and levying income tax which will then allow you to benefit from the double-taxation treaty between Holland and other areas. You should speak to a tax professional about that before you begin swashbuckling your way through these rather complicated treaties, but this is an option for someone who might be interested in these things.

While the tax climate may be favorable to people who do not work in the Netherlands, the industrial climate is not quite as favorable. The fact remains that you need to be able to get work offshore or be completely independently wealthy before you move to the Netherlands for any period of time. Because, even after you have secured a job in the Netherlands, your employer must prove that there is nobody who is a Dutch national who can do your job before you are allowed to keep your job beyond the third year.

This could be especially problematic for some people who do not have many skills or who just fall into a job temporarily and think that they have it for good. With a number of industrial-type industries as well as fishing and other chemical and electronics jobs, the Netherlands is not a place where exclusive work is found. The Netherlands is not a place where exclusive work is found. When deciding on making the Netherlands your offshore tax haven, this needs to be considered. Do you have savings which could theoretically last you months, if necessary? Or are you living paycheck to paycheck? Even if you have work which has been fairly consistent for several years, there really is no safeguard for you should you lose that work.

Switzerland

People often reflect longingly about Switzerland: the Swiss banks, the Swiss Alps, fine chocolate, and just about everything else that has to do with Switzerland. But do not be confused, because Switzerland is not a tax haven in the traditional sense of the word; tax rates can be as much as 30 percent in some areas.

The real benefit to living in Switzerland is what is known as their "fiscal deal," which is a tax deal that comes with a residence permit. Do not think that you can just walk onto the scene, though, grab a permit, and start down the slopes; it is not that easy. In fact, the Swiss are quite particular about who they allow to take advantage of these tax-saving opportunities. You need to become a resident, you cannot work or run a business from Switzerland, and you can be a Swiss national. This puts many people in a precarious conundrum, as even the most well-taken-care-of still need to make money somehow. There are ways around it for just about everybody, so you should have a look into the Switzerland solution and see what else is available.

Probably the smartest thing you can do is speak to somebody who is schooled in the matter. If you feel you qualify for residence in Switzerland, or if you just want to live there, then you should find out if you can submit an application. To qualify for the fiscal deal, though, you need to have a net worth of not less than 2 million Swiss francs, or $1.5 million. As you cannot run a business out of your home, this will make it much more difficult for people who are not independently wealthy. However, famous people for many years have been able to use the Swiss tax system to avoid paying taxes.

There are eight more taxes in Switzerland, including capital gains tax on property disposals (averaging 18 percent); social security (approximately 13 percent for employees), though this would not affect people using the fiscal deal because they cannot work; inheritance tax (in some situations); and a wealth tax (1.5 percent of the value of all your assets in Switzerland).

Switzerland is a great place to live, as people have known for some time. Switzerland is in the heart of Europe, there are relatively cheap properties to be had, crime is low, and the climate can be mild in many parts of the country, but the cost of living is very high.

For that matter, if you have a corporation in Switzerland, you are liable to pay the piper as well. A company is a resident in Switzerland if it was incorporated in Switzerland or if it is effectively managed from there. Resident companies need to pay tax on all of their worldwide income; nonresident companies only pay on profits which are generated from property in Switzerland.

Switzerland is perhaps best known for its banking system, which is among the most private and best run in the world.

San Marino

This tiny country which is fully entrenched in Italy is the perfect escape for somebody looking for something totally different and wanting to get away from all the tourism and other nonsense which goes along with many European countries. San Marino is only accessible by rail or road, making it not just quite isolated, but also very safe. But once you arrive you will probably agree that San Marino is one of the most unforgettable countries you will ever be able to visit.

Due to its excellent tourism industry as well as its banking, textiles, ceramics, cement, and wine production, San Marino is not only a beautiful place, but is also a thriving financial marketplace for your money and for the money of outside investors. For the interested individual looking for a second career in a specialty, later on in life, this may just be the place to set up shop.

Taxes are relatively low and if you are a nonresident investing in the country, investments are tax free. However, with a pretty high GDP and with a fairly exclusive, upscale resident base, San Marino may not be a great place for you to settle down. Costs of living drive even the best of us from perfectly legitimate places we called home.

San Marino is a great place to move to, and if you are able to look for opportunities to get into business ventures inside this thriving enclave, you should. Any business that would be able to make it to market in this region would have an excellent chance of doing well. If for no other reasons than their growing communications system and prosperous residents, San Marino may just be the best place outside of your home to set up shop and begin the second chapter of your life.

The United Kingdom

The United Kingdom comprises the areas known as Great Britain, Northern Ireland, Wales, and Scotland. The United Kingdom has a number of popular tax incentives for both residents and nonresidents to take advantage of.

There is a 0 percent personal income tax for all nonresidents. You will only be deemed a resident if you stay more than 182 days in any tax year, 91 days per tax year for four consecutive tax years, or if you visit so regularly and these visits are not accidental or due to an occasion. If you are a nonresident and you are in the U.K. you are only liable for income derived from property in the U.K., trade or profession undertaken in the U.K., or employment whose duties are performed in the U.K.

For this reason, many erstwhile travelers have been able to hole up in small nooks in the U.K. fabric and, as long as their trade is mobile or their income unlimited, people are able to have a great go of it in the United Kingdom. While being a transient is not for everyone and the gypsy went well out of style in a cultural context circa 1984, people are still able to live below the radar such that they are able to enjoy their lives without the intrusion of big government.

Also advantageous for people seeking offshore tax shelters are artists of particular persuasion. If you are a resident who is looking for some tax breaks forming a film partnership, you may get some shielding incentives to film. Neil Simon may have Brooklyn and Woody Allen is off the map, and there are undoubtedly numerous talented filmmakers who have been able to use the abandoned factories and workaday streets of London to great cinematic effect.

Also, if you are a resident nondomicile who has a foreign-sourced income, then that income is tax free. You just need to know the way to work the system in the U.K. and it can turn advantageous for even the most cynical of them all.

Just do not forget the subtext; the U.K. is forgiving, but overstay your welcome and it will be like the jaws of an alligator; if you linger too long, they will snap shut on your life and you will get a big tax bill. So the real story about the U.K. is that you have to declare and pay tax on your world income if you are a U.K. resident, so you should be sure to not overstay your welcome in any one of the three scenarios laid out above.

10

Africa

Many people considering their legal offshore tax haven may not think of the continent of Africa. With all the civil and social unrest which has existed there for years, and the disorganization and chaos which has overtaken the continent for decades, many would naturally find themselves looking elsewhere.

However, there are segments of Africa which may be worth your consideration for your offshore tax haven — even if it is in a hands-off fashion — as a place for you to incorporate an offshore business or open up a bank. There is a lot of growth going on in many different areas in Africa and this needs to be considered. While there is still much local infighting, there are many places which have moved past all that and have lived in relative peace for some time and have set up a communications infrastructure as well as a government infrastructure and are ready to move to the next level. This may be the place you are looking for when you are talking about your offshore tax haven.

Botswana

One place in Africa where you could be comfortable opening up a business may be in Botswana. There are many different types of business structures available in Botswana, such as limited liability corporations, external companies, companies limited by guarantee, partnerships, common law trusts, sole proprietorships, or societies (associations of persons). Company setup fees and costs are fairly low and can be advantageous for people looking to set up a company in Botswana.

With a good communication system and semiarid climate, this might also be the place for people to take up residence for part of the year. Just as long as you do not stay over 183 days in a year, you can live as a nonresident.

There are several corporate tax rates and personal tax rates which vary depending upon the taxable gains and taxable income that you receive, so you should be wary of that if you are looking for a completely tax-free existence. If you sell or otherwise dispose of your home, you will not be required to pay any taxes on the proceeds.

The country is stable and they have long since resolved their disputes with Gambia, Zambia, and Zimbabwe over boundary convergence and other issues. All in all, Botswana seems to be the perfect retreat for people looking to find a tax shelter and take up residence. Just be careful not to work there or earn an income and you will be able to avoid a majority of the resident taxes. You can also use an offshore trust to shelter your inheritance from taxes.

Liberia

Liberia may be one of the oldest tax havens in existence. It has no infrastructure and no local attorneys or accountants. The country of Liberia is merely in the business of registering corporations and registering ships. There are no services offered and most of the clientele who use Liberia as a tax haven actually never visit the country. There are companies registered there that have business carried out by representative offices in New York, Zürich, Hong Kong, Tokyo, and Rotterdam, among many others. If you are interested in registering your company, there are no taxes on offshore companies.

There are numerous security reasons people should not bank or live in this country. Liberia has unfortunately been the victim of many years of bloody civil wars, and rebels still control many parts of the small country. There is an unstable domestic infighting among rebel groups, youth gangs, warlords, insurgencies, as well as other street violence, looting, arms trafficking, ethnic struggles, and refugees from border areas.

The reason for this has deep roots and this is why their communication system is still poor and their organization and the whole country is still up in the air. While there is a 0 percent personal tax for nonresidents, even visiting there is ill advised because of all the security breaches.

Somalia

This is another example of a place you probably do not want to live in Africa. Due to the completely unstable social climate and the warring clans which occupy the various regions in the country, Somalia is a dangerous place for anyone to live. With literacy levels below 50 percent for men and below 25 percent for women, running a business is difficult. There is no unification in this country and the various clan leaders have a hard time agreeing on where their borders lie. While there is some effort to rebuild and gain some kind of stability within the country, the possibility of civil war breaking out at any moment is real.

That said, Somalia does have many advantages for people looking for tax breaks. If you incorporate a company there, you will be able to get a holiday from tax on the first three years. Following that initial period, you will only need to pay taxes on 50 percent of your profits. If you open up a bank, there is an annual charge of .25 percent on all deposits held in your bank.

So if you are looking for a cheap place to open your bank, and as long as your clients understand that your bank is going to be licensed in Somalia, you can open a bank there. Many Muslim clients will be comfortable to invest in Somalia due to the fact that the religious population in Somalia is near 100 percent Sunni Muslim. However, it should be noted that doing anything inside of Somalia is dangerous. In addition to the civil unrest which exists in Somalia, the climate is principally a desert and from December to February and May to October it is monsoon season. From May to October it there may be many hot and humid periods possible between monsoon seasons. There are also reccurring droughts, frequent dust storms, and floods during the rainy season.

South Africa

South Africa has many advantages to incorporating there. However, if you live there, South Africa will levy taxes on your world assets. You should also check the residency rules every year and keep an eye on what is going on because the rules are in flux. You can be a nonresident as long as you do not exceed 91 days a year for any three years in a row or do not spend 549 days there over any three years.

For personal tax, residents pay on an upward-sliding scale up to 40 percent, and residents who own special trusts will also pay up to 25 percent capital gains tax, and trusts from companies pay 50 percent capital gains tax.

There are numerous capital allowances which may be different from your current understanding of them, so you should make sure to look into them fully before you decide to make your move to South Africa. For example, buildings and other permanent structures do not qualify for wear and tear allowances, but you cannot claim capital allowances for expenditures on such things as hotels, patents, expertise, scientific research, trademarks, mining expenditures, agricultural capital, and other things.

There are also many public benefit organizations which may be able to make you exempt from tax. These organizations include things such as welfare and humanitarian organizations, health care, land and housing, education and development, religion, belief, philosophy, cultural, conservation, environment, animal welfare, research, consumer rights, or sports.

Popular businesses which are opened in South Africa include incorporated partnerships, limited to companies, trusts, and exempt companies, and international headquarters. South Africa has a good communication system, fairly stable social climate, and numerous banking opportunities. You should definitely consider this country if you are looking to move yourself into an offshore tax haven situation. Particularly if you are interested in growth, the future, or social welfare organizations; moving to South Africa may be just what you need.

Swaziland

Swaziland is one of the few countries in all of Africa which offers a genuine opportunity for people to live in a stable environment, relocate their businesses, and grow and flourish. If you are considering moving to Africa, Swaziland should be one of your top choices.

There are a few things about Swaziland which you should consider before you make the move over to this nation. One of these is that husbands and wives are taxed individually. If you are moving across and that is a consideration for you, then you should be aware of it. Income tax is only levied on Swaziland-source incomes and is on a sliding scale upward and can be as much as 30 percent.

If you are looking to go to Swaziland, you can only be there for 60 days without a visa and you need a work permit to work there. If you have a specialized skill which will benefit the country, getting a work permit should be fairly easy.

There are numerous duties and other taxes which need to be paid. Some of these include a 1.5 percent stamp duty on issues and transfers of shares; between 2 percent and up to 6 percent duty on land, buildings, and leases depending upon the value; a 10 percent nonresidents tax on interest whether individually or from your company; and a 37.5 percent tax on Swaziland-source profits for companies. An income is not taxed and there are no taxes on wealth, estates, or gifts. So if you are planning to operate an offshore business from Swaziland, this may be just the place to do it. You should be wary though, as Swaziland has entered into a number of double-taxation agreements with other places, most notably South Africa and the United Kingdom.

Far-Flung Tax Havens

There are a number of tax havens which are more remote, less thought of as tax havens, or more dangerous than other destinations. It is quite ironic, but fitting, that the most thought-of tax havens are islands; some would say perfect, relatively safe, low-tax, or tax-free societies which are like the popular boy or girl from high school: completely carefree and able to skate by on their good looks alone; great companions for a time, maybe forever.

Belize

For many people who do not know a great deal about what lies south of the United States, they may think that a country like Belize is just part of Mexico and is subjected to all the same rules as Mexico. But Belize is an independent country and it has some great advantages for people who are interested in a low tax payment or for investors who are working offshore or have the funds coming in from another source.

There is no capital gains tax and no inheritance tax in Belize. However, there is income tax and this can be a pretty intense experience for people who have to work there; as high as 45 percent in some cases. In addition, there are social security contributions that workers need to make, so if you are looking for a place to work, Belize probably is not your first choice.

However, for individuals who are residents but do not have a home there, the only tax is on income derived in Belize. Therefore, if you are an immigrant and you keep your money invested somewhere else offshore, you do not have to pay any income tax.

Even though buying property in Belize is fairly straightforward and there are no restrictions on foreigners who want to buy things there, you need to take the standard of living into account to decide if you want to live there at all. This is one of the least developed countries in the world and you should only consider it if you are able to subsidize your living and you want to be away from everything.

Belize also has the stigma of being a drug trafficking region of the world. That said, if you are morally averse to crime, then you may wish to consider elsewhere. Similarly, if you are heavily reliant on government services (which you are running away from paying taxes for) then you should probably not consider Belize.

Gibraltar

Occupying a mere 2.5 square miles in area and located at

the tip of Spain is a British territory known as Gibraltar. With a population of around 30,000 people and a good mixture of Maltese, English, Genoese, Italian, Spanish, and Jewish residents, Gibraltar is another great place for people to consider when they are looking for the most far-flung of offshore tax havens.

A part of the European Union and at the same time completely dependent on the United Kingdom, the area of Gibraltar has many challenges ahead of it. Despite the fact that the border between Gibraltar and Spain was reopened in 1985, talks remain "under discussion" for Gibraltar to become a Spanish territory, without any real progress. One of the only real concessions that people living in Gibraltar get is that they are excluded from a common external tariff, which is the common agricultural policy, as well as the requirement to levy the value added tax.

Despite the fact that personal tax can be high in Gibraltar, there are three types of companies that may be able to enjoy offshore tax savings in the territory of Gibraltar.

- **Nonresident Companies**—Companies incorporated in Gibraltar, but centrally managed and controlled by people who live outside of the jurisdiction, would fall under this category. If the company does not derive its income inside the territory of Gibraltar, then it is outside of the Gibraltar income tax. As an added bonus, companies incorporated inside of Gibraltar yet which fall under this category of company are not levied a flat-rate tax.

- **Tax-Exempt** — Even if your company does conduct business inside of Gibraltar, you may apply for tax-exempt status. Done after you incorporate and taking between 10 and 14 days, your company can receive an exemption certificate. This certificate is valid for 25 years and grants full exemption from income tax and any estate duties. All the participating company needs to do is pay a flat annual tax.

In order to more fully qualify for the tax-exempt status, your company does need to cede to a variety of conditions. For example, you cannot conduct trade in Gibraltar with another company unless it is tax exempt (exceptions are possible with prior consent). In addition there can be no changes in beneficial ownership, shareholders, or objectives without approval of authorities. The register of members needs to be maintained inside of Gibraltar, and no controlling interests may be held by residents of Gibraltar. Also, your annual tax fees are to be paid in equal installments split six months apart.

- **Qualifying Companies** — There are also some circumstances where tax needs to be remitted as a percentage of profits. You can get a certificate so that the tax will not waver, with only a few preconditions for obtaining a certificate.

There are also many benefits for formation of a company inside of Gibraltar, including the fact that there only needs to be two shareholders and two directors. You need to hold an annual general meeting of the shareholders inside of Gibraltar but any other meetings can be held anywhere else. You also need to work with an auditor who is registered under the Gibraltar Auditors Registration Ordinance in order to be claimed exempt. As another point of reference, you also need to have a registered office in Gibraltar to maintain company status there.

Gibraltar is a common-law jurisdiction and therefore is favorable for creating offshore trusts. While your trust needs to be registered, there is no income tax due on income derived outside of Gibraltar for a nonresident on trust income.

And Gibraltar is stepping up its game. The biggest draw to a place like Gibraltar is that they are looking more and more like an offshore finance center than ever before. There is a new office space and better communications, and Gibraltar is paring back its procedures and revving up its facilities so that it can be a tax-efficient base for offshore tax seekers.

Hong Kong

For Westerners, Hong Kong is something of a challenge to gain entry to in a beneficial manner. However, for people living in the Pacific, Hong Kong is a hot spot and one that continues to garner attention. This is of particular importance to people who have dual citizenship with an Eastern country and are tired of the heavy tax burden of the United States. Also, for people who are able to qualify for their nonresident Capital Investment Entrant Scheme, the benefits are pretty good. Finally, if you are a temporary worker in Hong Kong, not earning too much money and not giving any money to your children, there could be benefits for you as well. However, by and large, for Westerners there are not as many benefits besides the experience to draw a tax haven seeker out to this small peninsula.

Hong Kong has four airports, numerous ports, an excellent communications system, and a full industry of textiles, clothing, banking, shipping, electronics, plastics, toys, watches, and clocks. Hong Kong has numerous tourist attractions and the fact that Cantonese and English are both official languages makes a place like Hong Kong welcoming for tour groups as well as the intrepid individual.

For people already living in a nearby area in the Far East, Hong Kong has been described as a "Godsend" for the simple reason that a tax-free existence can be had in this nation so long as the money you earn is not from Hong Kong.

If you are wealthy and plan on investing some money in the Hong Kong economy then you may have the ability to live in Hong Kong rather comfortably. However, there are certain criteria you need to pass, including 1) be 18 years or older, 2) have net assets of no less than HK $6.5 million at the time of your application submission, 3) have invested or plan to invest HK $6.5 million with the Immigration Department, 4) have no adverse record from Hong Kong or from your home country, and 5) be able to display that you are capable of supporting yourself while you are in the country without the assistance of anyone else.

The final tax beneficiary of the Hong Kong tax burden is the employee who is working less than 60 days in Hong

Kong; then their salary is exempted from Hong Kong taxes. If your stay is longer than 60 days, you are still able to take advantage of the tax allowances, related to the amount of time that you spend in Hong Kong beyond those 60 days.

For the worker, the confusion begins when discussion about the tax laws starts to get particular. For example, if you are a guest worker and your employer is providing housing, this is taxed to the employee at 10 percent of their total wages. Also, if you are making any "employee child payments," those are taxable. You may wish to have these terms more clearly defined if you think you are taking a quick, tax-free jaunt on assignment through the Orient. You do not want to find out that all that money you thought you would make is in fact taxable; if your services are needed enough, you should be able to have your employer reimburse you once you get back to your home country.

Labuan

As a small, east Malaysian island in the South China Sea, Labuan is going to be one of those places that you wish you had looked into a lot sooner, because, as of 1990, the Malaysian government set up Labuan as an international offshore financial center, which many people have already taken advantage of. Fortunately for you though, Labuan has not attracted a great deal of attention, so it is still a good place worth examining if you are looking at forming an offshore tax haven.

Offshore trading companies pay 3 percent on profits or a fixed sum of around $5,000, whichever is lower. If you take the step to form an investment or nontrading company, you will not pay any tax at all. However, for many people privacy is paramount, so if that is what you need, then you can pay the minimum fixed-sum amount and then you do not need to file anything.

There are no disclosure requirements in Labuan either and all gains tax, making Labuan an excellent spot for you to try to form your offshore tax haven. Noted for being even a step up from its overseeing neighbor, Malaysia, Labuan is one of the top choices for people looking to migrate east for tax haven purposes. Due to intense cultural shifts from traditional Western ideas, it may not be for everyone. But if you are of Eastern descent or if you are willing and capable to learn the customs, traditions, language, and life style, Labuan may just be the place for you.

Lebanon

As an offshore tax haven, Lebanon is a great place for an investor to consider. People considering investing in Lebanon should remember a couple of different things before they decide to locate their companies there. While the stability in the area has been in place since 1976 with Syrian troops along their border, there is always the stigma of doing business in the Middle East and the potential for tempers to erupt.

Another thing to consider is that you should not manufacture or provide financial services through your offshore company in Lebanon lest you be subjected to the corporate tax that businesses are levied.

One more thing to consider is that seeking citizenship in Lebanon is not recommended. Lebanon still operates on the military draft system, so if you are considering seeking citizenship or if you have children of that age, they could end up having to serve in the Lebanese army.

Many people may think that Lebanon is strictly a Middle Eastern country; however, there are a number of languages which are spoken in Lebanon including French, English, as well as Armenian and Arabic. There are eight airports into and out of the nation of Lebanon.

With a number of popular industries in the nation, there are numerous opportunities for doing just about anything you want to: banking, food processing, jewelry, cement, textiles, mineral and chemical products, furniture products, oil refineries, and metal fabrication are just as some of the numerous industries which take place within Lebanon's borders.

However, with the good communications system and mild weather, Lebanon may just be the place for you to set up some sort of an offshore tax shelter. Offshore companies receive extra-special tax treatment in Lebanon, so long as they do not participate in manufacturing, banking, insurance, holding, industrial practices, or any commercial activity within the Lebanese territory. At the time of the writing of this book, there is a $600 flat-rate charge on offshore companies, and they are subjected to 6 percent capital gains tax.

Malaysia

With the booming economy in the Orient and the rapid growth going on in Eastern nations all the time, it should surprise no one that Asian nations are interested in having business in their neck of the woods. It should also be noted, though, that with the growing and changing economy in the East, it is important to realize that what you read in this book today could change rapidly.

However, the southeastern Asian country of Malaysia has long been known for its great deals in terms of business. Many of the Malaysian business incentives include things like investment tax allowances for businesses such as manufacturing companies, high-technology companies, tourist development, and research and development. There are also income tax incentives for people living in Malaysia as well as double-deduction tax allowances. There are also tax incentives for operational headquarters and Malaysian shipping companies, so if you are considering either basing your business out of this Asian country or creating a shipping company there, you have reason to expect tax deductions.

Similarly, if you run a business inside of Malaysia but you generate income from outside of Malaysia, you are free from tax, except in the instance of banking institutions, insurance companies, or sea and air transport companies.

There are 117 airports in this nation and it is a fairly volatile climate with flooding, landslides, and forest fires all threatening your well-being. Despite that fact, people continue to move to Malaysia and there is a good communications system. If you are looking to use Malaysia as a launching point for your tax-free existence, you have to remember that you can enjoy nonresident tax allowances just as long as you do not stay more than 182 days in any calendar year.

Netherlands Antilles

As a place to form an offshore tax haven, the Netherlands Antilles is one which needs to be looked at with some restraint. The simple reason is this: the Netherlands Antilles is set to be disbanded on December 15, 2008. This means the area is definitely in flux and is liable to be so for some time. Even though they have the strong support of each other and of nations like the United States, we will have to see what this disbandment will do to this area.

As of the writing of this book, there is no centralized government just because of the fact that all these disparate islands all call each other neighbor. It looks like the Netherlands Antilles could be a great place for you to stay if you were going to be using your boat tour to enjoy an offshore tax haven. It is right in the Caribbean Sea and it is near other islands, so you could enjoy the tax-free status of a nonresident for 90 days in the Netherlands Antilles and then go somewhere else.

If you stay any longer than 90 days, you need to apply for permanent residency. Part of this application process involves declaring an amount which will be large enough for you to sustain yourself for the rest of your time in this country. Once you have declared this sum of money, then you will be taxed on any income derived from this sum. Furthermore, this tax haven levies taxes on your entire world income and you could be subject to double taxation if you have citizenship elsewhere.

Panama

Another Central American country which is close to Costa Rica and shares many of the same tax breaks is Panama. Panama is one of the most well-established tax havens in the land, and not only because of its tax breaks, but also because it is regarded by many as an excellent place to live. There is no tax on income earned outside of Panama, so just like Costa Rica and other areas, the tax system is territorial. This is quite common for Central and South American countries, such as Nicaragua, Paraguay, Guatemala, and Bolivia; as long as you do not have any locally earned income, these are all excellent options for you to move to and set up your tax-free status.

You should be wary of people who try to lure you to someplace that has policies you are not familiar with. Brazil, Peru, Ecuador, Chile, Mexico, Colombia, and Venezuela all will tax you in full, so you should be careful of the borders which surround you. If you are told that the same policies apply to your living in another country, then be careful— it is not necessarily true that the same tax policies will apply.

Even though capital gains are counted as income, if your capital gains are from an overseas company, then this is also tax free. However, if you do any personal or corporate business within the confines of Panama City, they will be subject to taxation. The tax rate can be near 30 percent.

In terms of low cost-of-living, though, Panama is among the most well known. It is inexpensive on a number of other fronts and thus popular. There are beautiful three-bedroom beachfront homes available for around $200,000 or less. Contrary to popular opinion, the cost of living here is around one quarter of the cost of living in the United States, and Panama is known as one of the safest places in the world to live.

Despite the tropical climate, Panama is not inside the hurricane belt, so you are less likely to see any damaging tropical storms.

Another benefit to moving to Panama is the ease with which they allow you to do so. If you are an interested foreigner who wants to move to the country, there are provisions which will allow you to prove that you have a guaranteed income of $500 a month or $600 for a married couple and that is it. Once you have qualified to become entitled for residency, you will get a passport and be able to enjoy discounts to all sorts of things such as travel, meals, and even hospital discounts.

In general, Panama is a good value for what you are paying. There are also many incentives for people to move to Panama, including political stability, privacy laws, and strong business foundations.

Qatar

Due to its relative proximity to Saudi Arabia and the volatile social climate which surrounds it, many would think that a place like Qatar is about as far flung as you could get and that you would want to be as far away as possible from this area of the world. The fact is quite the opposite, as the Qatari military has done a number of good things in the past years, has helped the United States military, has thwarted a coup in 2002, and has made the country as safe as anywhere else in the world.

Qatar is particularly popular with Pakistanis, Arabs, Yemenis, and Indians. This could have to do with a 95 percent Muslim population and the fact that anybody can avoid income tax in Qatar as long as their income source is not in Qatar. In fact, Qatar is a good choice for Muslims and Westerners alike as it has a low tax and is a stable and wealthy country for people to reside in.

The personal income tax is 0 percent for all nonresidents. People who live there and work there pay income tax on a sliding scale. But the people who live in Qatar tend to be wealthy, so the fact that they pay a lot in taxes is a relative thing based on percentage.

Another good thing about the peninsula area of Qatar is that there is 0 percent corporate tax on nonresident corporations. For corporations that call Qatar their home, the taxes go up on a similar sliding scale. Corporations that earn less than QR 100,000 are tax exempt and corporations that earn between QR 100,001 and QR 500,000 only pay a 10 percent income tax. It goes up from there to the 35 percent ceiling on corporations that earn QR 5,000,001 and above, but there are a number of allowable deductions for things such as interest payments, rentals, salary, bonuses, depreciation, losses from the sale of assets, humanitarian deductions, scientific donations, and other fees besides income tax. So, as you can see, the Qatar government is lenient on corporations who are bringing money and jobs to their area.

12

Reality Versus Fiction: Common Misperceptions

It is also necessary to dispel any myths. For this reason it is important we get the messy inaccuracies out of the way before we examine specifics any further.

Foreign-earned income exclusion caveats: There are numerous bars you have to pass, or periods of time that must have elapsed, before you are able to claim outright exclusion up to stated limits:

- The limits for the earned income exclusion are $70,000 for the individual and $140,000 for the married couple who are both earning income. Even if one of you makes considerably more than the other, it is only $70,000 per person; a wife who earns $100,000 and a husband who earns $40,000 are still only able to claim $110,000 for these rules.

- Your tax home is the location of your place of business. However, if you maintain a place of residence in the United States, even if you principally work and live part time in another country, your place of residence is still considered the United States.

- You need to establish residency in the foreign country at least 330 days of one year in order to qualify for the $70,000 offshore tax exemption.

- Offshore tax havens are not just for the rich. Many average American citizens go to foreign countries and live like kings.

- If you are an American citizen living in another country, not working and not earning income, you still have to file your federal income tax. Even if your income is zero, you still need to file an income tax return as long as you retain your American citizenship.

13

Benefits

The primary benefits of participating in legal offshore tax havens are relative to your individual situation. However, there are also other tangible benefits to this process which should be explored for both the business and the individual.

The biggest benefit to utilizing the offshore tax haven is not having to pay taxes. If you are comfortable with the fact that you may not have the government to fall back on when you are old, then this may be the kind of thing for you. Even if you just do it for a couple of years to travel, see the world, and then come back and establish residency in the United States, you can shield a great deal of your assets from taxation. We will learn about that a little later on, because there are simple steps you can take to make sure money is not something that the federal government and the IRS can get their hands on.

With the current state of the world and with the United States in a perilous position, now may be as good a time as any to investigate this option. If you could go somewhere in the world where there is peace, where you do not have a big bureaucracy trying to shove its rules down your throat, and where you can live your life and be free, why would you not want to do that?

This seems to get back to the central tenets of the offshore tax haven. Americans seem to be moving toward an offshore tax shelter as a way of revolting against their government. Anyone who draws parallels back to the 1700s, with tossing tea into Boston Harbor and "taxation without representation," is missing the point.

People are fed up with what they consider to be irrelevant social programs, wasteful government spending, sloppy bureaucracy, and other apparent vices in the American system. If you are a person who is seeking freedom from taxes, you are not alone. The fact of the matter is that many Americans in particular are tired of the big government trying to do too much and not holding the proper people accountable. The American taxpayer is feeling less and less represented by a government rife with earmarks and special interests. As one of the pair of the only things certain in life, it would appear that all Americans, save the very well connected, are essentially in the same boat.

So another big benefit of the offshore tax haven is self-reliance: being able to take your life into your own hands and earn and be paid what you are worth. The offshore tax haven could be for anybody who earns any amount of money, including freelance writers or other contractors.

The offshore tax haven is traditionally for disaffected individuals who are self-reliant and are interested in living in a foreign country. An individual from the United States who is interested in participating in the offshore tax haven game needs to maintain his residence 11 months out of the year, so his first year outside the United States is often void just because people's lives do not necessarily restart on the first of January. There are also a number of bars a person needs to reach to qualify for the benefits of offshore tax haven status. However, people who make a great deal of money can tell you that 30 to 40 percent of their income going out the window is something that they scowl upon. Once the money has been made and invested in proper outlets, people often feel like they would rather live a comfortable life somewhere else; so they do.

Tax havens also have another benefit for the people who are fed up with Big Brother trying to step into their lives and run their whole program. Too often in big-government countries, there is a natural inclination to want to know everything about all the money people make; nowhere is this more prevalent than in the United States. For this reason, many expatriates are seeking to have the government leave them alone and not even ask about their financial status, let alone demand to know everything about every penny they earn.

Tax haven countries typically are sensitive to personal information and never overstep their boundaries when it comes to people who live there and their financial matters. With this sharp contrast — from 30 to 40 percent of your money being taken away by the government to none of your money even being asked about by the government — it is easy to see why many people view this as a much better living situation.

Effects

So many people would like to take advantage of legal offshore tax havens, and well they should. However, one must consider the long-term effects of this decision. What about your next-of-kin's status as a citizen? What happens if you want to return? What is the process? What type of penalties could be imposed on people who walk away from the tax code for several years and want to return? These are all important questions to remember when you are considering participating in a legal offshore tax haven.

While it may be legal, there are definitely repercussions which extend well beyond the initial bliss of being tax free. These are things which need to be considered before you embark on the journey of an offshore tax haven.

14

The IRS

The fact that Americans are trying to escape their tax burden is not lost on the Internal Revenue Service or the American federal government. They are always trying to catch crooks, as well they should. However, the practices discussed in this book are all legal. While citizens of the United States need to pay taxes, there are a growing number of people who are taking an alternative route.

Two out of three people who move offshore end up not staying current on their taxes. The IRS has a prevailing interest to see that these tax crooks are brought to justice or that their citizenship is taken from them. With numbers this high, it is not surprising that the IRS is trying to crack down on people who are living abroad. Expatriates put a great deal of trust in foreign governments with the hope that their identity will not be revealed and that they will be able to live freely away from the grasping arms of their home country. However, people who are interested in leaving their own country would be wise to do things properly to avoid headaches and possible legal procedures down the road.

Many people may look to this book and wonder, "Why does the IRS matter? Are they not the ones I am trying to eliminate from my life?" While that is true, you should do so the right way and you should be able to parse the distinctions. For example, in legal terms there is a huge difference between "tax avoidance" and "tax evasion." One involves any and all legal means to minimize your tax burden while the other implies using illegal means to do the same.

If you utilize the services of a CPA and are able to classify whatever expenses you believe are legitimate business deductions to try to reduce your net income, this is legal. Even when the IRS disagrees with you, as a business person you will never have to fear indictment, seizure of property, shutting down of your business, and jail time for doing this. At the worst you will just be forced to pay what you thought you would not have to.

However if you knowingly and of your own free will do not report income, fail to comply with procedures, or try to skirt out of the reach of the law, or act in an illegal manner, then you are evading your tax burden. This is illegal.

Similarly, when you are trying to establish yourself as a resident of another country to get out of the tax man's reach over here, you should do things the right way so that you have nothing to fear. Being foolish is the worst thing you can do in the tax world because there are harsh penalties which carry minimums and leave no room for first-time offenders. Saving a few hundred or even a few hundred thousand dollars is not, to most people, worth the possibility of 15 years of their life in prison. If you are going to lessen or eliminate your tax burden, you should always do it the right way and make sure all your actions are above board.

Become a Nonresident

Many people who plan on leaving the United States so that they do not have to pay taxes are able to do so by becoming a nonresident elsewhere. There are a number of rules to this; the biggest of these is that the individual interested in doing so must give up his or her citizenship and forfeit residency in the United States for at least 330 days per year or 11 months out of 12. When you have done this, you take on the tax burden of the country that you are living in, be it bigger or smaller. This is one reason you want to fully investigate a potential host country and find out all of the particulars before you take the plunge.

An individual is able to take on the residence of another country by establishing what is known as "bona fide" residence. This status, also known as "Non-Resident Qualified Individual," offers the advantage of relief on the first $80,000 of foreign-earned income. An individual may be able to further use these tax treaties to their advantage by offering some assistance on their foreign capital gains, pension income, and other U.S. income. Another bonus is that housing expenses are able to be deducted when they pass the threshold of more than $7,000 per year.

There are a number of things which you have to be wary of when you are trying to avoid taxes from Big Brother. Being a part-time resident of the world is a tough thing to keep track of and you need to make sure the country that you are living in has not changed their rules, because even if they amend their policies after you have renounced your citizenship, you still need to play by their current rules.

We are all slaves to our employer, our government, our courts, our police, and sometimes even our spouse. If you are ready to give all that up and become invisible to the world at large, then you are part of a growing consensus among people who have had enough of big government trying to tell them what they can and cannot do. However, you need to be careful, you need to be vigilant, and you need to understand what you are getting yourself into because entering into anything any other way is a fool's game.

Conclusion

With all this information, you may begin to feel swamped and wonder where to go to learn more. In the appendices that follow, there are numerous resources listed which were used in compiling this book. You should also look over much of the specific information for the tax haven you are considering utilizing. Speak with someone who is schooled in this variety of planning and who will have a definite opinion on your most beneficial course of action.

The tasks laid out in front of you may seem arduous. It may seem like all this work will be for naught, as you will not even notice the benefits for years to come. While it is true that there are many expenses involved in taking your whole life and moving it off to another continent, the opposite could be argued in that it may appear to be such a waste living in a high government state and flushing all your money away toward a social services system that seems likely to be dissolved soon, and which benefits only the rich and the poor.

It would seem that there are a number of things which need be taken into account before you are able to make an accurate summation as to the viability and plausibility of the legal offshore tax haven as a plan of attack for your own personal fortunes. While there are many preconceptions flying around, many of these are found to be false. You also need to remember that the differences between neighboring countries are great when it comes to tax burdens. There are some nations you could be seeking out as a tax shelter and then find that the place may end up being nothing of the kind; your tax break could end up costing you more in headaches and in finances than you may have ever imagined.

However, the facts remain that many people in high tax lockdowns like the United States are fed up with all the money wasted blithely which does not work for them. They feel their money is just a part of an expansive, expensive government Gestapo which has sent others screaming for the door before you; now it is your turn.

Legal offshore tax shelters are a real thing and they represent real value for tens of thousands of the richest and savviest people who have found their way around the system. If you feel that your adventuresome spirit has never died and that you are ready, willing, and able to make a go of it, then press on. Make the legal offshore tax shelter not just a temporary blip across your financial radar but a permanent change which will benefit you and yours to come in smart and bountiful ways.

Appendix A

There are a number of great organizations all over the world that can help you with further information about different tax haven regulations in their different countries.

The U.K. and Ireland

Tax Consultants Fund
Info Guide Publications, Ltd.
Mayfair House
14-18 Heddon St.
Mayfair, London
W1B 4DA
Telephone: 0871 5045532
info@taxconsultantsguide.com

Citycas Ltd.

Valiant House
4-10 Heneage Lane
London   EC3A 5DQ
Telephone: 0207 626 7171
Fax: 0207 626 7272
info@citycas.com

Clark & Co.

12 North Hill
Colchester, Essex
CO1 1AS
Telephone: 01206 577422
Fax: 01206 562816
partners@clarke-colchester.co.uk

MD Consulting Limited

St Mary's Court
The Broadway
Amersham
Buckinghamshire
HP7 0UT
01494 772765

Taxation Web Ltd.
6 Coleby Avenue
Peel Hall
Manchester
M22 5HH
United Kingdom
Mark McLaughlin
martino@taxationweb.co.uk

Berg Kaprow Lewis
35 Ballards Lane
London
Greater London
N3 1XW
England
Telephone: 020 8922 9222
Fax: 020 8922 9223

Bartlett Kershaw Trott
4 Pullman Court, Great Western
Road
Gloucester
Gloucestershire
GL1 3ND
England
Telephone: 01452 527000
Fax: 01452 304585

The Wells Partnership
The Old Rectory, Church Street
Weybridge
Surrey
KT13 8DE
England
Telephone: 01932 704 700
Fax: 01932 855 049

Greenwood Barton
National Westminster Bank
Chambers
Heckmondwike
West Yorkshire
WF16 0HU
England

Harris Lipman
2 Mountainview Court, 310 Friern
Barnet Lane
Whetstone
London
N20 0YZ
England
Telephone: 020 8446 9000
Fax: 0208446 9537

Maskell, Moss, & Co. Limited
24 Cathedral Road
Cardiff
South lamorgan
CF11 9LJ
Wales
Telephone: 029 2025 6330
Fax: 029 2025 6331

The Institute of Chartered
Accountants in Ireland
CA House, 87/89 Pembroke Rd.
Dublin
Ir 4
Ireland
Telephone: +353 1 63 7200
Fax: + 353 1 6680842

Isle of Man
Isle of Man – Head Office
OCRA (Isle of Man) Limited
Grosvenor Court
Tower Street
Ramsey, Isle of Man IM8 1JA
British Isles
Telephone: +44(1624) 811000
Fax: +44(1624) 811001
Email: Stevenson@ocra.com
Contacts: David Stevenson, Colin
Forster, Brian Monk

Conway, Conway & Co.
12 Basin St
Nass
Co. Kildare
KD, Ireland

Italy

Faulkner International Ltd. Rome
Vio Carlo Passaglia No 11
Rome, Italy
Senior Financial Consultant
Email: johnmpye@faulkner-
international.com

Faulkner International Ltd. Turin
Piemont
Turin, Italy
Financial Consultant Email:
david.silk@faulkner-international.
com

Mary Jan Bridges
Telephone: 06474-7069
Address: Via Urbana 116, 00184
Rome

Donald J. Carroll
Telephone: 06570-281
Fax: 06570-282733
Address: Largo Angelo Fochetti
28, 00154 Rome
Email: donald.carroll@
studiopirola.com

Cynthia J. Ehrlich
Telephone: 06336-0340
Address: Via Cassia 595/F, 00189
Rome
Email: USTAXhelp@yahoo.com

Timothy Ellis
Telephone: 06614-3216
Address: Via Paolo V 11 – Int. 7,
00167 Rome

Vincent P. Gambino
Telephone: 063751-1192 Fax:
063741-1420
Address: Via Asiago 1, 00195
Rome
Email: VPGambino@tiscalinet.it

Sally M. Silvers
Telephone: 06853-57172
Address: Via Basento 37, 00198
Rome
Email: sally.silvers@flashnet.it

France

Faulkner International Ltd. Paris
Faulkner Counseil SARL
116, Avenue du General Leclerc
75014 Paris
France
Email: info@faulkner-international.
com

**Faulkner International Ltd.
Valbone**
Faulkner Conseil SARL
6, Rue Soutrane, 1er Etage
06560 Valbonne
France
Regional Director
email: terry.hurley@faulkner-
international.com

Czech Republic

**Faulkner International Ltd. Czech
Republic**
p.a. On-Target
Perlova 1 110 00 Prague 1
Czech Republic
Financial Consultant Email: david.
newton@faulkner-international.
com

Germany

Tax Consultants Guide
Info Guide Publications
Lindenstrasse 2
Glenhausen
Frankfurt
Germany
63571
Phone: +49 6051 618140
Email: info@taxconsultantsguide.
com

Brazil

Faulkner International Ltd. Brazil
Rua Haddock Lobo 846
Conjunctura 1105
Edificio Netware
Cerqueira Cesar
01414-000 Sao Paulo
Brazil
Regional Director email: robin.
saunders@faulkner-international.
com
Consultant email: info@faulkner-
international.com

Faulkner International Ltd. Brazil
Traversa do Ouvidor 50 (sobreloja)
Centro 20040 – 040 Rio De Janeiro
Brazil
Regional Director
Email: timrichards@faulkner-
international.com
Web site: **http://faulkner-
international.com**

Norway

**Faulkner International Ltd.
Norway**
Proffice, Lokkeveien 10,
400 Stavaner,
Norway
Email: ian.neil@faulkner-
international.com,
steve.calloway@faulkner-
international.com

The Netherlands

Faulkner International Ltd.
Netherlands, Eindhoven
Faulkner Nederland BV
Fellenoord 130, 5611ZB
Eindhoven
Netherlands
Email: info@faulkner-international.
com

Faulkner International Ltd.
Netherlands, Hoofddorp
Faulkner Nederland BV
De Horsten, Planetenweg 15A
2132HN Hoofddorp
Netherlands
Financial Consultant Email:
clive.anderton@faulkner-
international.com

Vietnam

Faulkner International Ltd.
Vietnam
Ho Chi Minh City
Vietnam
Financial Consultant Email: keith.
bridger@faulkner-international.
com

Bahrain

Faulkner International Ltd.
Kingdom of Bahrain
Manama
Kingdom of Bahrain
Regional Director Email: chris.
watts@faulkner-international.com

Latvia

Faulkner International Ltd. Latvia
Latvia
Email: into@faulkner-international.
com

Russia

Faulkner International Ltd.
Moscow
Moscow
Email: info@faulkner-international.
com

Dubai

Faulkner International Ltd Dubai
Apt 307, Obedulla Tower
PO Box 52465
Bur Dubai
Dubai
United Arab Emirates
Regional Director Email: eric.
boardman@faulkner-international.
com

Thailand

Faulkner International Ltd.
Thailand
Bamboo Court Apartment 5
59-38 Sukumvit Soi 26
Klongtoey
Bangkok 10110
Thailand
Regional Director Email: john.
macgill@faulkner-international.com

China

Faulkner International Ltd. China,
Shenzhen
1 Gong Ye 1st Rd
Shekou Industrial Zone
518069 Shenzhen
The People's Repulic of China
Email: info@faulkner-international.
com

Faulkner International Ltd. China, Shanghai
14C No:1051, Xin Zha Road
Jing An District
Shanghai 200041
The People's Republic of China|
Regional Director Email:
brian.mcandrew@faulkner-international.com

OCRA (Hong Kong) Limited
3908 Two Exchange Square
8 Connaught Place
Central
Hong Kong
Telephone: +852 2522 0172
Fax: +852 2522 4720
Email: hongkong@ocra.com.hk
Bart Dekker
Iris Les

Korea

Faulkner International Ltd. Korea Seoul
Korea
Email: info@faulkner-international.com

Japan

Faulkner International Ltd. Japan
9F Motoakasaka Building
1-7-10 Motoakasaka
Minato-Ku
Tokyo, 107-0051
Japan
Financial Consultant Email:
asher.lepcha@faulkner-international.com

Switzerland

Faulkner International Ltd. Switzerland, Geneva
MPM Geneva (European International Office)
Avenue Louis-Casai 18
1211 Geneva 28
Switzerland
Email: info@faulkner-international.com

Faulkner International Ltd. Switzerland, Basel
Basel
Switzerland
Email: info@faulkner-international.com

Spain

Faulkner international Ltd. Spain

World Trade Center
Edifico Sur – 2a Planta
Muelle de Barcelona
Barcelona, 08039
Spain
Regional Director Email: paul.
evans@faulkner-international.com
Training Manager Email: steve.
carter@faulkner-international.com

Australia

Ten-Forty Tax Preparation

P.O. Box 988
Bondi Junction, NSW 1355
Richard Grilliot
Email: tenforty@bigpond.net.au

Expatriate Tax Associates

1 Grove Street
Birchgrove, NSW 2041
Email: evanhill@extax.com.au
www.extax.com.au
Telephone: 9555-5663
Fax: 9810-0557

Taylor Woodings Corporate Services

Level 26 Royal Exchange Building,
56 Pitt Street
Sydney, NSW   1225
Telephone: (02) 8247 8000
Fax: (02) 8247 8099

Price Waterhouse Coopers

201 Kent St.
Sydney, NSW 2000
GPO Box 4177
Sydney, NSW 2001
Jim Tait: 8266-2992
Helen Cudlipp: 8266-2995
Carol Separovich: 8266-5769
Rohan Geddes: 8266-7261
Fax: 8266-8910

Walter Jacenko

P.O. Box 247
Eastwood, NSW 2122
Telephone: 9874-4558
Fax: 9874-6440

Ernst & Young

321 Kent Street
Sydney, NSW 2001
G.S. Choong or Ron Crowe
Telephone: 9248-5555
Fax: 9248-5314

U.S. Tax Management P/L
1907/1 Sergeants Lane
St. Leonards, NSW 2065
Al Simpson
Email: alsimpson@bigpond.com
Telephone: 9906-2633
Fax: 9906-2644

KPMG
KPMG Centre
45 Clarence St.
Sydney, NSW 2000
GPO Box H67 Australia Square
Sydney, NSW 2000
Rodney Moor
Telephone: 9335-8202
Fax: 9299-7077

Darrel Casubrook
Causbrook & Associates
Suite 1204, Level 12
66 King Street
Sydney, NSW 2000
Email: darrel.causbrook@
causbrooks.com.au
Telephone: 9299-1850
Fax: 9299-1860

Richard A. Bobb
155 Castlereagh Street
7th Floor
Sydney, NSW 2000
Richard Bobb or Kathryn Chow
Telephone: 9261-2422
Fax: 9264-8701

Deloitte Ross Tohmatsu
255 George Street
Sydney, NSW 2000
C.J. Getz
Telephone: 9322-7680
Fax: 9322-7025

Harry V. Turner & Co.
Suite 25
105 Longueville Rd.
Lane Cove, NSW 2066
P.O. Box 673
Lane Cove, NSW 1595
Harry Turner
Telephone: 9427-0599 or 9427-0818
Fax: 9427 – 5976

Teresea D. West
C/- Cropper Parkhill
Solicitors
Level 20, 1 Castlereagh Street
Sydney, NSW 2000
(P.O. Box 71 Burwood, NSW 2134)
Mobile: 0418-681-284
Telephone: 9232-5000

Duthre Samurai & Co. Pty Ltd.
Charles A Duthie
P.O. Box 97
Lane Cove, NSW 2066
Telephone: 9418-6942
Fax: 9418-6855
Web site: **www.dsco.info**

John L. Campbell
c/o Zein el Hassan
Corrs Chambers Westgarth
Governor Philip Tower
Sydney, NSW 2000
John L. Campbell
Telephone: 9210-6500
Fax: 9210-6611
(for estate and gift taxes only)

Australian Capital Territory
Duesburys Chartered
Accountants
7th Floor St. George Bank Building
60 Marcus Clarke Street
Canberra, ACT 2601
GPO Box 500
Canberra, ACT 2601
Telephone: 02-6279-5400
Fax: 02-6279-5444
Michelle Horner – US Tax
Specialist

Hallett and Company
Level 8 AMP Tower
1 Hobart Place
Canberra, ACT 2602
Telephone: 02-6257-5712
Fax: 02-6257-5958
Peter Radford – US Tax Specialist

Queensland KPMG
345 Queen Street, Level 30
Brisband, Qld 4000
GPO Box 223
Brisbane, Qld 4001
Bill Armagnacq
Telephone: 07-3233-3111
Fax: 07-322-0074

Perth
The Tax Lady
5 Malcom Court
Noranda, WA 6062
Telephone: **08-9375-5946**
Email: marv@starwon.com.au

United States

U.S. Accounting Associations
www.taxsites.com/associations2.
html#accounting-us

American Bar Association
Section of Taxation
www.abanet.org/tax/home.html

American College of Trust and
Estate Counsel
www.actec.org

American Institute of Certified
Public Accountants
www.aicpa.org

American Payroll Association
www.americanpayroll.org

American Property Tax Counsel
www.aptcnet.com

American Society of
IRS Problem Solvers
www.irsproblemsolvers.com

American Taxation Association
www.atasection.org

American Association of America
www.appraiserassoc.org

Association for Computers and
Taxation – **http://taxact.org**

Center for State and Local
Taxation – **www.irg.ucdavis.
edu/csltax.html**

Council on State Taxation
www.statetax.org

Federation of Tax Administrators
www.taxadmin.org

Institute for Professionals in
Taxation – **www.ipt.org**

Multistate Tax Commission
www.mtc.gov

National Association of
Computerized Tax Processors
www.nactp.org

National Association of Enrolled
Agents – **www.naea.org**

National Association of State
Auditors, Comptrollers and
Treasurers – **www.nasact.org**

National Association of State
Budget Officers – **www.nasbo.org**

National Association of Tax
Consultants – **www.natctax.org**

National Association of Tax
Professionals – **www.natptax.com**

National Council of Property
Taxation – **www.ncpt.net**

National Society of Tax
Professionals – **www.nstp.org**

National Tax Association
www.ntanet.org

National Taxpayers Conference
www.statetaxes.net

Tax Executives Institute
www.tei.org

U.S. State Tax Associations

Alabama Society of EAs
Roland Fricke, EA
P.O. Box 242
Arab, AL 35016
Phone: 256-586-4111
Fax: 256-586-4138
Email: buddy@bara.net
Web site: **www.alsea.org**

Alaska Society of EAs
H. Joi Soucy, EA
P.O. Box 2163
Kodiak, AK 99615
Phone: 907-486-6225
Fax: 907-486-4129
Email: msbear@worldnet.att.net

Arizona Society of EAs
Larry Martin, EA
7360 E 22nd St #109
Tucson, AZ 85710
Phone: 520-722-8363
Fax: 520-722-8398
Email: martinea@juno.com
Web site: **www.aztaxpros.org**

Arkansas Society of EAs
Sherry Main, EA
15493 Riches Rd
Fayetteville, AR 72704
Phone: 479-521-0310
Fax: 479-521-2269
Email: slmain@nwark.com
Web site: **www.arksea.org**

California Society of EAs
Richard J Quarterman, EA
13204 Myford Road Ste 835
Tustin, CA 92782-9118
Phone: 949-261-2111
Fax: 949-261-7070
Email: r.quarterman@att.net
Web site: **www.csea.org**

Colorado Society of EAs
Victoria Bell, EA
6535 S. Dayton Street
Englewood, CO 80111
Phone: 303-708-8077
Fax: 303-708-8079
Email: bellsultax@aol.com
Web site: **www.taxpro.org**

CSEA Executive Office:
Catherine Apker, CAE
Executive Vice President
3200 Ramos Circle
Sacramento, CA 95827
Phone: 916-366-6646
Fax: 916-366-6674
Email: evp@csea.org

Connecticut Society of EAs
Caroline Frano, EA
1111 E Putnam Ave.
Riverside, CT 06878
Phone: 203-637-3887
Email: caroline.frano@snet.net

Florida Society of EAs
Lynn Schmidt, EA
1495 Sixth Street, SE
Winter Haven, FL 33880
Phone: 863-295-9895
Fax: 863-298-8299
Email: lynn@lyncotax.com
Web site: **www.fseaonline.org**

FSEA Executive Office:
Jean Gates EA
P.O. Box 3895
Clearwater, FL 33767
Phone: 727-442-2806
Fax: 727-442-2724
Email: taxtiger@gte.net

Georgia Society of EAs
Audrey L. Griffin, EA
Griffin Tax Service
100-C N. Houston Lake Blvd
Centerville, GA 31028-1713
Phone: 478-953-5016
Fax: 478-953-6092
Email: griftax@grifsolu.com
Web site: **www.4gaea.org**

Hawaii Society of EAs
David Ramirez, EA
P.O. Box 61397
Honolulu, HI 96839-1397
Phone: 808-589-2322
Fax: 808-589-2422
Email: irstaxrelief@msn.com

Illinois Society of EAs
Karen Miller, EA
496 W. Boughton Road
Bolingbrook, IL 60440
Phone: 630-759-5070
Fax: 630-759-9101
Email: eataxes@aol.com

Illinois Society of EAs
Executive Director: Jacquelie
Meyer, EA
1415 Matanuska Trail
McHenry, IL 60050
Phone: 815-385-6889
Fax: 815-363-1623
Email: Meyer_JD@msn.com

Indiana Society of EAs
Helen (Casey) Juza, EA
202 E Main Street
Danville, IN 46122
Phone: 317-745-6051
Fax: 317-745-1735
Email: execserv@aol.com
Web site: **www.**
indianaenrolledagents.com

Iowa Society of EAs
David J Adkins, EA
4415 Stone Ave.
Sioux City, IA 51106
Phone: 712-276-9240
Email: Jeff@adkinstax.com

Kentucky Society of EAs
John C Frazier, EA
8333 Alexandria Pike Ste. 204
Alexandria, KY 41101
Phone: 859-694-3000
Fax: 859-448-2762
Email: jctaxpro@aol.com

Louisiana Society of EAs
Dexter Duhon, EA
114 S. State Street
Abbeville, LA 70510
Phone: 318-893-2702
Fax: 318-893-2780
Email: djd@msis.net

Maryland/DC Society of EAs
Robert Jacobs, EA
550M Ritchie Hwy, #145
Serverna Park, MD 21146
Phone: 410-544-4680
Fax: 410-544-1324
Email: ataxguru@prodigy.net

Massachusetts Society of EAs
Leon M. Rudman, EA
39 Powell Street
Stoughton, MA 02072
Phone: 781-344-9031
Fax: 781-344-9031
Email: rudman@comcast.net
Web site: **www.maseaonline.org**

Michigan Society of EAs
Robert Hemenway, EA
602 West Main Street
Owosso, MI 48867
Phone: 989-723-5977
Fax: 989-725-8372
Email: hbsowosso@michonline.
net

MiSEA Administrative Office
1071 E Nine Mile Rd
Hazel Park, MI 48030
Phone: 248-547-9934
Fax: 248-547-9934

Minnesota Society of EAs
Dorothy Anderson, EA
P.O. Box 748
Crosslake, MN 56442
Phone: 218-692-2650
Fax: :218-692-3364
Email: aceinc@crosslake.net
Web site: **www.mnsea.org**

Mississippi Society of EAs
Bertha Page, EA
615 West Canal Street
Picayune, MS 39466-3916
Phone: 601-798-3116
Fax: 601-798-5650
Email: pagetax@datasync.com

Missouri Society of EAs
James Bales, EA
1800 Liberty Park Blvd, #6
Sedalia, MO 65301
Phone: 660-827-3212
Email: taxpro@iland.net
Web site: **www.naea.org/mosea**

Nevada Society of EAs
Cherene D. Cooper, EA
2585 S. Jones Blvd, Ste 2D
Las Vegas, NV 89146-5604
Phone: 702-646-4646
Fax: 702-364-4697
Email: cherene.cooper@gte.net

New Mexico Society of EAs
Linda Ruckel, EA
3900 Paseo del Sol
Santa Fe, NM 87507
Phone: 505-988-9572
Fax: 505-988-9572
Email: advancetax1@cs.com

New Jersey Society of EAs
Martin Stein, EA
11 New York Blvd
Edison, NJ 08820
Phone: 732-548-8023
Fax: 732-548-8023
Toll Free Referral Line: 866-652-6232
Email: martystax@aol.com
Web site: **www.njsea.org**

New York State Society of EAs
Sandra Martin, EA
15 Reitz Pkwy
Pittsford, NY 14534
Phone: 585-381-8585
Fax: 585-442-8252
Email: pats1040@aol.com
Web site: **www.nyssea.org**

North Carolina Society of EAs
Louis Arthur, EA
7610 Falls of The Neuse Road
Suite 100
Raleigh, NC 27615
Phone: 919-844-6488
Fax: 919-844-6460
Email: larthur@nbt-cpa.com
Web site: **www.nc-sea.org**

Northern New England
Society of EAs
David Landers, EA
P.O. Box 331
Rye, NH 03870
Phone: 603-964-7177
Fax: 603-964-9030
Email: taxmayvin@aol.com

Ohio State Society of EAs
Nancy Remus, EA
2901 Wexford Blvd
Stow, OH 44224
Phone: 216-673-0463
Email: nremus@aol.com
Web site: **www.ossea.org**

Oregon Society of EAs
Peter Mar, EA
P.O. Box 23402
Eugene, OR 97402
Phone: 541-607-9200
Fax: 541-607-1770
Email: peter@helpmytaxes.com

Oklahoma Society of EAs
Leslie Armstrong, EA
2000 S. Douglas Blvd
Midwest City, OK 73130
Phone: 405-741-0832
Fax: 405-737-7600
Email: leslie@armstrongtax.com

Pennsylvania Society of EAs
George Meyers, EA
677 West DeKalb Pike
King of Prussia, PA 19406
Phone: 610-337-2220
Fax: 610-265-7801
Email: gjmea@aol.com

Rhode Island Society of EAs
D.J. Hadden, EA
27 Whipple Avenue
Westerly, RI 02891
Phone: 401-596-6179
Fax: 401-596-6179

South Carolina Society of EAs
Lawrence G Picard Sr., EA
400 Stratford Drive
Summerville, SC 29485-8642
Phone: 843-871-1065
Fax: 843-871-1332
Email: larrypicard@knology.net

Tennessee Society of EAs
Caryle M. Breeden, EA
7345 Middlebrook Pike
Knoxville, TN 37909
Phone: 865-963-4274
Fax: 865-531-1846
Email: tnigot2go@aol.com

Texas Society of EAs
Louis Powell, EA
408 W College Street
Carthage, TX 75633
Phone: 903-693-7491
Fax: 903-693-7492
Email: louispowel@aol.com
Web site: **www.txsea.org**

Utah Society of EAs
Dave Sheldon, EA
9449 Union Square #200
Sandy, UT 84070
Phone: 801-571-2870
Fax: 801-571-2891
Email: daveshel@concentric.net
Web site: **www.utsea.org**

Virginia Society of EAs
J. Michael Boyle, EA
P.O. Box 7246
Richmond, VA 23221
Phone: 804-565-8055
Fax: 804-565-8055
Email: j4m9b9@aol.com
Web site: **www.vaeas.org**

VASEA Executive Director: John
M. (Mike) Hall
13208 Sherri Drive
Chester, VA 23831-4540
Phone: 804-748-4733
Fax: 804-748-2318
Email: va.sea@verizon.net

Washington State Society of EAs
Linda Shipway, EA
16605 152nd Place NE
Woodinville, WA 98072
Phone: 425-483-2956
Email: linda.shipway2@verizon.net
Web site: **www.taxea.org**

WSSEA Administrative Office:
Mariaane Kreycik, EA
222 E Fourth Ave, Suite A
Ellensburg, WA 98926
Phone: 509-925-6931
Fax: 509-962-5807
Email: taxpro@ellensburg.com

Wisconsin Society of EAs
Diane M. Lotto, EA
200 South Washington St.
Green Bay, WI 54301
Phone: 920-432-6466
Fax: 920-432-5751
Email: dlotto@tds.net

WiSEA Executive Office:
Donald Wollersheim, EA,
Executive Director
115 East Waldo Blvd.
Manitowoc, WI
Phone: 920-684-6940
Fax: 920-684-8208
Email: donw@lsol.net

Other Resources

International Tax Associations
Interarntional Accounting
Associations
www.taxsites.com/associations2.
html#international

Ad Concordiam
http://www.adconcoridian.net

Canadian Payroll Association
http://www.payroll.ca

Canadian Property Tax
Association
www.cpta.org

Canadian Tax Foundation
www.ctf.ca

Canadian Taxpayers Federation
www.taxpayer.com

Chartered Institute of Taxation
U.K. – **www.tax.org.uk**

Council for International Tax
Education – **www.fdta-cite.org**

European-American Tax Institute
www.eati.co.uk

European Association of Tax Law
Professors – **www.eatlp.org**

FSC/DISC Tax Association
www.fdta-cite.org

Institute for Fiscal Studies – U.K.
http://www1.ifs.org.uk

Institute of Taxation in Ireland
www.taxireland.ie

Inter-American Center of Tax
Administrations – **http://ciat.org**

International Association of
Assessing Officers
www.iaao.org

International Fiscal Association
www.ifa.nl

U.S. Branch
www.ifausa.org

International Tax Planning
Association – **http://itpa.org**

North American Society of
Tax Advisors
www.taxadvisors.com

Swedish Taxpayers Association
www.skattebetalarna.se

Taxation Institute of Australia
www.taxinstitute.com.au

Taxpayers Association of Europe
www.taxpayers-europe.org

Taxpayers Australia
www.taxpayers.com.au

Appendix B

The following is a list of offshore countries that have little or no taxes.

- Andorra
- Anguilla
- Antigua and Barbuda
- Aruba
- Bahamas
- Bahrain
- Barbados
- Belize
- Bermuda
- British Virgin Islands
- Canary Islands
- Cayman Islands
- Cook Islands
- Costa Rica
- Cyprus
- Dominica
- Dominican Republic
- Gibraltar
- Grenada
- Guernsey

- Isle of Man

- Jersey

- Liberia

- Liechtenstein

- Maldives

- Malta

- Marshall Islands

- Mauritius

- Monaco

- Montserrat

- Nauru

- Netherlands Antilles

- Niue

- Panama

- Samoa

- Western Samoa

- San Marino

- Seychelles

- St. Lucia

- St. Kitts and Nevis

- St. Vincent and the Grenadines

- Switzerland

- Tonga

- Turks and Caicos

- U.S. Virgin Islands

- Vanuatu

Appendix C

The following is a list of states and their religions.

Catholic Nations

Nations which recognize Catholicism as the official religion:

- Argentina

- Bolivia

- Costa Rica

- El Salvador

- Holy See (Vatican)

- Paraguay

Protestant Nations

Nations which recognize a form of Protestant Christianity as their official religion:

- Vanuatu

- Samoa

- United Kingdom

Islamic Nations

Nations which recognize Islam as their official religion:

- Afghanistan

- Algeria

- Bangladesh

- Comoros

- Libya

- Mauritania

- Morocco

- Iran

- Iraq

- Jordan

- Malaysia

- Maldives

- Oman

- Pakistan

- Saudi Arabia

- Tunisia

Buddhist Nations

Nations which recognize Buddhism as their official religion:

- Bhutan

- Burma

- Thailand

Hindu Nations

Nations which recognize Hinduism as their official religion:

- Nepal

Appendix D

The following is a list of Bahamian Banks:

Atlantic Bank of Commerce Limited

http://www.firstatlanticcommerce.com
P.O. Box N8865
Nassau, N.P., The Bahamas
Telephone: 242-326-0740
Fax: 242-325-1272
Deputy General Manager: Mrs. Hilda Knowles

BankAmerica Trust and Banking Compan

http://www.bankofamerica.com
BankAmerica House
East Bay Street, P.O. Box N-9100
Nassau, Bahamas
Telephone: 809-393-7411
Fax: 809-393-3030
Telex: 20 159

Bankers Trust Company

Claughton House
P.O. Box N-3234
Nassau, Bahamas
Telephone: 809-325-4107

Bank of Bahamas Limited

http://centralbankbahamas.com
50 Shirley Street, P.O. Box N-7118
Nassau, Bahamas
Telephone: 809-326-2560
Fax: 809-325-2762
Telex: 20141 BBL

Bank of Boston Trust Company Limited

Charlotte House
P.O. Box N-3930
Nassau, Bahamas
Telephone: 809-322-8531
Telex: 20189 BOSTRUST

Bank of Nova Scotia

http://www.scotiabank.com/cda/content/0,,CID50_LIDen,00.html
Box N-7545 Bay Street
Nassau, Bahamas
Telephone: 809-322-4531
Fax: 809-328-8473
Email: 19163288473@faxsav.com

Bahamans Offshore Accounts

http://bahamas-offshoreaccounts.com

Barclays Bank in the Bahamas

http://www.bahamas.barclays.co.uk/off-bahamas.html
Full range of banking services

Chemical Bank & Trust Limited

http://www.chemicalbankmi.com
P.O. Box N-4723
Nassau N.P., The Bahamas
Telephone: 242-322-1003
Fax: 242-326-7339
Senior Trust Officer: Mr. Michael Ranson

CIBC Trust Company

http://www.cibc-global.com/jur_bah_frm.html

Cititrust Bahamas

http://www.citibank.com
Thompson Boulevard P.O. Box -1576
Nassau, Bahamas
Telephone: 809-322-4240
Fax: 809-325-6147
Telex: 20420

Coutts & Company Limited

http://www.couts.com/contact/bahamas.asp
P.O. Box N7788
Nassau, N.P., The Bahamas
Telephone: 242-326-0404
Fax: 242-326-6709
Manager: Mr. James D. Graham

Darier Hentsch Private Bank & Trust Limited

http://www.darierhentsch.com/darier/nassau.htm

P.O. Box N4983

Nassau, N.P., The Bahamas

Telephone: 242-322-2721

Fax: 242-326-6983

Vice President: Mrs. Anna Colebrooke

Demachy Worms & Co. International

P.O. Box N3918

Nassau, N.P., The Bahamas

Telephone: 242-326-0282

Fax: 242-326-5213

Financial Controller: Mr. Ronald W. Springle

Eastland American Bank Limited

P.O. Box N4920

Nassau, N.P., The Bahamas

Telephone: 242-325-9170

Fax: 242-325-1002

Manager: Mr. Tyrone Fowler

Euro-Dutch Trust Co. Limited

P.O. Box N9205

Nassau, N.P., The Bahamas

Telephone: 242-325-1033

Fax: 242-323-7918

Managing Director: Mr. Anthony L.M. Inder Rieden

Fidinam Trust Corporation Limited

P.O. Box N9932
Nassau, N.P., The Bahamas
Telephone: 242-326-5084
Fax: 242-328-0541
Resident Manager: Mr. Cedric B. Moss

Guta Bank & Trust Limited

http://www.interknowledge.com/bahamas/investment/guta-bank/
index.html

Laurentian Bank & Trust Company Limited

http://www.laurentianbank.com
P.O. Box N4883
Nassau, N.P., The Bahamas
Telephone: 242-326-5935
Fax: 242-326-5871
Managing Director: Mr. E. Andre Doyon

Lloyds Bank International Private Banking

http://www.lloydstsb.com
P.O. Box N4843
Nassau, N.P., The Bahamas
Telephone: 242-322-8711
Fax: 242-322-8719
Telex: 20107 BOLAM
Assistant Manager, Trust Department: Mr. Sam P. Haven

Mees Pierson Limited

http://www.meespiersonci.com
P.O. Box SS5539
Nassau, N.P., The Bahamas
Telephone: 242-393-8777
Fax: 242-393-0582
Managing Director: Mr. Geoffrey Dyson

Montaque Securities International Limited

http://www.montaquesecurities.com

Saffrey Square

Bay Street & Bank Lane, 1st Floor
P.O. Box N7474
Nassau, N.P., The Bahamas
Telephone: 242-356-6133
Fax: 242-356-6144
President & Managing Director: Owen S.M. Bethel

Morgan Trust Company of The Bahamas

http://www/morimor.com
P.O. Box N4899
Nassau, N.P., The Bahamas
Telephone: 242-326-5519
Fax: 242-326-5520
Managing Director: Mr. Andrew G Massie

Offshore Trust Banking Corporation Limited

West Bay Road, P.O. Box N7179
Nassau, Bahamas
Telephone: 809-322-4585
Telex: 20111

Rawson Trust Company Limited

P.O. Box N4465
Nassau, N.P., The Bahamas
Telephone: 242-322-7461
Fax: 242-326-6177
Manager, Accounts: Mrs. B.M. Rolle

Royal Bank of Canada

http://www.rbcprivatebanking.com/tier3_bahamas.html

Royal Bank of Scotland (NASSAU) Limited

http://www.royalbankscot.co.uk
Box N3045, 50 Shirley Street
Nassau, Bahamas
Telephone: 242-322-4643
Fax: 242-326-7559
Email: 19163267558@faxsave.com

Sand Ander Investment Bank Limited

P.O. Box N1682
Nassau, N.P., The Bahamas
Telephone: 242-322-3588
Fax: 242-322-3585
Manager: Mrs. R. L. Symonette

The Private Trust Corporation Limited

http://www.privatetrustco.com

The Chase Manhattan Private Bank

http://www.chase.com
P.O. Box N1576
Nassau, N.P., The Bahamas
Telephone: 242-323-6811
Fax: 242-326-8814
Unit Trust Department: Mrs. Eunice E. Smith Manager

The Citibank Private bank

http://www.citibank.com
P.O. Box N1576
Nassau, N.P., The Bahamas
Telephone: 242-323-3521
Fax: 242-323-6147
Managing Director: Mr. David N. Tremblay

Thorand Trust & Management Limited

P.O. Box N3242
Nassau, N.P., The Bahamas
Telephone: 242-393-8622
Fax: 242-393-3772
Managing Director: Mr. Robert V. Lotmore

Westpac Bank & Trust (Bahamas) Limited

http://www.westpac.com.au
P.O. Box N8332
Nassau, N.P., The Bahamas
Telephone: 242-328-8064
Fax: 242-326-0067
Managing Director: Mrs. Jacqueline M. Bain

Appendix E

The following is a list of St. Lucian Banks.

Bank of Novia Scotia. The

6 WM Peter Blvd/
Box 301, Castries
St. Lucia
758-456-2100

Bank of Novia Scotia. The

Rodney Bay
Gross Islet
St. Lucia
758-452-8805

Bank of Novia Scotia. The

Cnr Chausee Rd. & High St.
Castries, St. Lucia
758-452-3797

Barclays Bank Plc

Bridge St
Box 335
Castries, St. Lucia
758-456-1000

Bank of Novia Scotia. The

New Dock Rd.
Box 223, Vieux Fort
St. Lucia
758-454-6314

Barclays Bank Plc.

Customer Services
Castries, St. Lucia
758-456-1125

Barclays Bank Plc.

Operations Department
Castries, St. Lucia
758-456-1118

Barclays Bank Plc.

Manager Operations,
Castries, St. Lucia
758-456-1104

Barclays Bank Plc.

Barclays Bank Hotline
Castries, St. Lucia
758-451-8009

Barclays Bank Plc.

Foreign Business
Castries, St. Lucia
758-456-1142

Barclays Bank Plc.

Business Centre
Castries, St. Lucia
758-456-1008

Barclays Bank Plc.

Senior Corporate Manager
Castries, St. Lucia
758-456-1002

Barclays Bank Plc.

Manager Corporate Centre
Castries, St. Lucia
758-456-1003

Barclays Bank Plc.

Small Business Manager
Castries, St. Lucia
758-456-1006

Barclays Bank Plc.

Business Banker
Castries, St. Lucia
758-456-1123

Barclays Bank Plc.

Area Manager
Castries, St. Lucia
758-456-1101

Barclays Bank Plc.

Merchant Services
Castries, St. Lucia
758-452-2642

Barclays Bank Plc.

Manager Personal Banking
Castries, St. Lucia
758-452-4115

Barclays Bank Plc.

Personal Bankers
Castries, St. Lucia
758-456-1158

Barclays Bank Plc.

Vieux Fort
St. Lucia
758-454-6255

Barclays Bank Plc.

Manager
St. Lucia
758-454-6914

Barclays Bank Plc.

Rodney Bay Marina
Gross Islet, St. Lucia
758-452-9384

Barclays Bank Plc.

Insurance Broking
Barfincor, St. Lucia
758-453-2015

Barclays Bank Plc.

L'Anse Rd.
Castries, St. Lucia
758-452-4999

Barclays Bank Plc.

Apartment
Castries, St. Lucia
758-452-3347

Barclays Bank Plc.

Sports Club
Castries, St. Lucia
758-451-8259

Caribbean Banking Corporation Ltd.

Micoud St., Box 1531
Castries, St. Lucia
758-452-2265

Caribbean Banking Corporation Ltd.

Gablewoods Mall
Vieux Fort, St. Lucia
758-451-7469

Caribbean Banking Corporation Ltd.

Gablewoods Mall South
Vieux Fort, St. Lucia
758-454-7264

Cibe Caribbean Ltd.

Wm Peter Blvd.
Box 350
Castries, St. Lucia
758-456-2422

Cibe Caribbean Ltd.

Fredrick Clark St
Vieux Fort, St. Lucia
758-454-6262

Eastern Caribbean Central Bank

Financial Centre
Bridge St, Box 295
Castries, St. Lucia
758-452-7449

First Citizens Bank

www.firstcitizenstt.com
St. Lucia
868-623-2576

National Commercial Bank of St. Lucia Ltd.

Financial Centre Building
1 Bridge Street
Box 1860
Castries, St. Lucia
758-456-6000

National Commercial Bank of St. Lucia Ltd.

Bridge St. Branch
Box 1862
Castries, St. Lucia
758-456-6000

National Commercial Bank of St. Lucia Ltd.

Waterfront Branch
Box 1031
Castries, St. Lucia
758-456-6000

National Commercial Bank of St. Lucia Ltd.

Vieux Fort Branch
Box 261
Vieux Fort, St. Lucia
758-454-6327

National Commercial Bank of St. Lucia Ltd.

Southfriere Branch
Box 243
Soufriere, St. Lucia
758-459-7450

National Commercial Bank of St. Lucia Ltd.

Gros Islet Branch
Box 2046
Gros Islet, St. Lucia
758-450-8002

National Commercial Bank of St. Lucia Ltd.

Bureau De Change
Hewanorra Intl. Airport
Vieux Fort, St. Lucia
758-454-7780

Royal Bank of Canada

Wm Peter Blvd
Box 280
Castries, St. Lucia
758-452-2245

Royal Bank of Canada

Audit Dept
Box 280
Castries, St. Lucia
758-451-9463

Royal Bank of Canada

Rodney Bay Marina
Gros Islet, St. Lucia
758-452-9921

Royal Bank of Canada

New Dock Rd.
Vieux Fort, St. Lucia
758-454-5804

Royal Bank of Canada

Business Banking Centre
Castries, St. Lucia
758-450-3951

St. Lucia Co-operative Ltd.

G F L Charles Airport
Castries, St. Lucia
758-451-8482

St. Lucia Co-operative Ltd.

JQ'S Mall
Rodney Bay, St. Lucia
758-452-8882

St. Lucia Co-operative Ltd.

Commercial St.
Box 342
Vieux Fort, St. Lucia
758-454-6213

St. Lucia Co-operative Ltd.

17 Bridge St.
Box 168
Castries, St. Lucia
758-455-7000

St. Lucia Co-operative Ltd.

George F L Charles Airport
Box 168
Castries, St. Lucia
758-451-8842

Appendix F

The following is a list of banks in the U.K.

Internet & Telephone Banking Current Accounts

Cahoot Abbey National
http://www.cahoot.co.uk

Barclays Internet Banking
http://ibanking.barclays.co.uk

Co-op Internet Banking Smile
http://www.smile.co.uk

EGG
http://www.egg.com

Intelligent Finance
http://www.if.com

Woolwich
http://www.openplan.co.uk

Lloyds TSB
**http://www.lloydstsb.com/
services/internet**

Bank of Scotland
http://www.bosinternet.com

First-e
http://www.first-e.com

Virgin
http://www.virgin-direct.co.uk

Internet Savings Bank
http://www.imbd.com

High Street Banks & Building Societies With High Street Branches Throughout the UK for Savings & Banking

Abbey National High Street Bank
http://www.abbeynational.co.uk

Barclays High Street
http://www.barclyas.co.uk

Cheltenham & Gloucester
http://www.cheltglos.co.uk

Alliance and Leicester
http://www.alliance-leicester.co.uk

Bristol & West
http://www.bristol-west.co.uk

Bradford & Bingley
http://www.bradford-bingley.co.uk

Britannia
http://www.brittannia.co.uk

Co-Op
http://www.co-operativebank.co.uk

Halifax
http://www.halifax.co.uk

HFC
http://www.hfcbank.co.uk

HSBC Midland Highstreet Bank
http://www.hsbc.com

Lloyds TSB
http://www.lloydstsb.co.uk

Nationwide
http://www.nationwide.co.uk

Natwest Branches
http://www.natwest.co.uk

Royal Bank of Scotland
http://www.rbs.co.uk

Portman
http://www.portman.co.uk

Woolwich Building Society
http://www.woolwich.co.uk

Yorkshire
http://www.ybs.co.uk

Other Banks and Building Societies

Bank of England
http://www.bankofengland.co.uk

Bank of Ireland
http://www.bank-of-ireland.co.uk

Bank of Scotland
http://www.bankofscotland.co.uk

Bank of Wales
http://www.bankofwales.co.uk

Barnsley
http://www.barnsley-bs

Beverley
http://www.beverleybs

Birmingham
http://www.
birminghammidshires.co.uk

Cambridge
http://www.cambridge-building-
society

Capital Bank
http://www.capitalbank.co.uk

Cash Centres Ltd.
http://www.cashcentres.co.uk

Carter Allen
http://www.carterallen.co.uk

Catholic
http://www.catholicbs.co.uk

Century
http://www.century-building-
society

Charterhouse
http://www.charterhouse.co.uk

Chelsea
http://www.thechelsea.co.uk

Chesham
http://www.cheshambsoc.co.uk

Cheshire
http://www.chershirebs.co.uk

Citibank
http://www.citibank.co.uk

Clay Cross
http://www.claycross.co.uk

Coinco International
http://www.coinco.co.uk

Coutts
http://www.coutts.com

Darlington
http://www.darlington.co.uk

Derbyshire
http://www.thederbyshire.co.uk

Dudley
http://www.
dudleybuildingsociety.co.uk

Dunfermline
http://www.dunfermline-bs.co.uk

Earl Shilton
http://www.esbs.co.uk

Ecology
http://www.ecology.co.uk

ECU Group
http://www.ecu.co.uk

Express Finance
http://www.express-finance.
co.uk

First Trust Bank
http://www.fibni.co.uk

Flemming
http://www.flemmin.co.uk/
premier

Furness
http://www.furnessbs.co.uk

Gainsborough
http://www.gbbs.demon.co.uk

Hambros
http://www.hambrosbank.com

Hamilton
http://www.hdb.co.uk

Hanley Economic
http://www.thehanley.co.uk

Harpenden
http://www.harpendenbs.co.uk

Hays
http://www.hays-banking.co.uk

Hinckley and Rugby
http://www.hrbs.co.uk

ICC Bank
http://www.icc.ie

Ilkeston Permanent
http://www.ipbs.co.uk

Ipswich
http://www.ipswich-bs.co.uk

Kent Reliance
http://www.krbs.co.uk

Lambeth
http://www.lambeth.co.uk

Leeds & Holbeck
http://www.leeds-holbeck.co.uk

Leek
http://www.leek-united.co.uk

Legal & General
http://www.landg.com

Lombard
http://www.lombard.co.uk/
banking

Loughborough
http://www.theloughborough.
co.uk

Manchester
http://www.themanchester.co.uk

Mansfield
http://www.mansfieldbs.co.uk

Market Harborough
http://www.mhbs.co.uk

Marsden
http://www.marsdenbs.co.uk

Melton Mowbray
http://www.mmbs.co.uk

Mercantile
http://www.mercantile-bs.co.uk

Newbury
http://www.newbury.co.uk

Newcastle
http://www.newcastle.co.uk

Northern
http://www.nbonline.co.uk

Norwich & Peterborough
http://www.npbs.co.uk

Nottingham
http://www.notthingham-bs.co.uk

Personal Loan Corporation
http://www.loancorp.co.uk

Principality
http://www.principality.co.uk

Progressive
http://www.theprogressive.com

Prudential
http://www.pru.co.uk

Saffron Waldon Herts
http://www/swhebs.co.uk

Salomon Brothers
http://www/sbil.co.uk

Scarborough
http://www.scarboroughbs.co.uk

Scottish
http://www.scottishbldgsoc.co.uk

Shepshed
http://www/theshepshed.co.uk

Skipton
http://www.skipton.co.uk

Spanish/Gibraltar
http://www.npbs-gibraltar.co.uk

Stafford Railway
http://www/srbs.co.uk

Staffordshire
http://www/
staffordshirebuildingsociety.
co.uk

Standard Bank
http://www.sbl.co.uk

Standard Chartered
http://www.stanchart.com

Standard Life
http://www.standardlifebank.com

Stroud & Swindon
http://www.stroudswindon.co.uk

Swansea
http://www.swansea-bs.co.uk

Teachers
http://www.teachersbs.co.uk

Tridos
http://www.tridos.co.uk

Appendix G

The following is a list of Swiss banks:

- A &A Actienbank

- ABB Export Bank

- ABN AMRO Bank (Schweiz)

- ABN AMRO Bank N.V. Amsterdam

- AIG Private Bank Ltd.

- ANZ Grindlays Bank Ltd.

- AP Anlage & Privatbank AG Bach

- Aargauische Kantonalbank

- Adler & Co. AG

- Alpha Rheintal Bank

- Alternative Bank ABD

- Amas Bank (Switzerland) Ltd.

- American Express Bank (Switzerland)

- Amtserssparniskasse Oberhasli

- Amtserssparniskasse Schwarzenbu

- Amtserssparniskasse Thun

- Anker Bank

- Appenzeller Kantonalbank

- Arab Bank (Switzerland) Ltd.

- Aramd von Ernst & Cie. AG

- Artesia (Suisse) SA

- Arzi Bank AG

- Atlantic Vermogensverwaltungsbank

- BB Bank Belp

- BBVA Privanza Bank (Switzerland) Ltd.

- BDL Banco di Lugano

- BEKB BCBE

- BFC Banque Financiere de la Cite

- BGG Banque Genevoise de Gestion

- BHF Bannk (Schweiz) AG

- BLP Banque de Oirtefeyukkes

- BNP Paribas (Suisse) SA

- BS Bank Schaffhausen

- BSI SA

- BZ Bank Aktiengesellschaft

- Banca Arner SA

- Banca Commerciale Italiana (Switzerland)

- Banca Commerciale Lugano

- Banca Euromobiliare (Suisse) SA

- Banca Monte Paschi (Suisse) SA

- Banca Popolare di Sondrio (Suisse) SA

- Banca Privata Edmond de Rothchild Lugano SA

- Banca Unione di Credito

- Banca del Ceresio SA

- Banca del Gottardo

- Banca del Sempione

- Banca dello Stato del Cantone Ticino

- Banca di Credito e Commercio (BANKREDIT)

- Banco Espirito Santo SA

- Banco Mercantil (Schweiz) AG

- Banco Santander Cenrtal Hispano (Suiza) SA

- Bank Adamas AG

- Bank Austria Cerditanstalt (Schweiz) AG

- Bank Butschwil

- Bank CIAL (Schweiz)

- Bank Coop

- Bank EEK

- Bank Ehinger & Cie.

- Bank Eschenback

- Bank Hapoalim (Schweiz) AG

- Bank Hofman AG

- Bank Hugh Kahn & Co. AG

- Bank J. Vontobel & Co. AG

- Bank Jacob Safra (Schweiz) AG

- Bank Julius Bar & Co. AG

- Bank Leerau

- Bank Leu AG

- Bank Leumi le-Israel (Schweiz)

- Bank Linth

- Bank Morgan Stanley AG

- Bank Sal. Oppenheim Jr. & Cie.

- Bank Sprasin & Cie.

- Bank Sparhafen Zurich

- Bank Thorbecke AG

- Bank Wartau-Sevelen

- Bank am Bellvue

- Bank for International Settlements

- Bank fur Handle & Effekten

- Bank im Thal

- Bank in Gossau

- Bank in Huttwil

- Bank in Langnau AG

- Bank in Zuzwil

- Bank of America National Association

- Bank of New York – Inter-maritime Bank

- Bank of Tokyo – Mitsubishi (Schweiz) AG

- Bank von Ernst & Cie. AG

- Banque Alerienne du Commerce Exterieur SA

- Banque Audi (Suisse) SA

- Banque Banorient (Suisse)

- Banque Baring Brothers (Suisse) SA

- Banque Bonhote & Cie. SA

- Banque Bruxelles Lambert (Suisse) SA

- Banque CAI Caisse Alfa Banques

- Banque Cantonale Neuchateloise

- Banque Cantonale Vaudoise

- Banque Cantonale de Fribourg

- Banque Cantonale de Geneve

- Banque Cantonale du Jura

- Banque Cantonale du Valais

- Banque Degroof Luxembourg SA

- Banque Diamantaire Anversoise (Suisse) SA

- Banque Edourad Constant SA

- Banque Franck SA

- Banque Francaise de l'Orient (Suisse) SA

- Banque Galland & Cie. SA

- Banque General du Luxembourg (Suisse) SA

- Banque International de Commerce BRED

- Banque Ippa & Associates, Luxembourg

- Banque Jenni & Cie. SA

- Banque Jurassienne d'Epargne et de Credit

- Banque Labouchere SA

- Banque MeesPierson Gonet SA

- Banque Multi Commercials

- Banque Nationale de Paris (Suisse) SA

- Banque Notz Stucki SA

- Banque Pasche SA

- Banque Piguet & Cie. SA

- Banque Privee Edmond de Rothschild SA

- Banque SCS Alliance SA

- Banque Syz & Co. SA

- Banque Tardy de Watteville & Cie. SA

- Banque Thaler

- Banque Unexim (Suisse) SA

- Banque Vontobel Geneve SA

- Banque Worms (Geneve) SA

- Banque de Camondo (Suisse) SA

- Banque de Commerce et de Placements SA

- Banque de Depots et de Gestion

- Banque de Gestion Financiere BAGEFI

- Banque de Patrimoines Prives Geneve BPG SA

- Bantleon Bank AG

- Barclays Bank (Suisse) SA

- Basellandschafliche Kantonalbank

- Banque Cantonale de Bale

- Baumann & Cie

- Bayeriche Landesbank (Schweiz) AG

- Benrnberg Bank (Schweiz) A

- Bezirks-Sparkasse Dielsdorf

- Bezirkskasse Laufen

- Bezirkssparkasse Uster

- Biene – Bank im Rheintal

- Bordier & Cie

- Burgerliche Ersparniskasse Bern

- C.I.M.Banque

- CBG Banca Privata Lugano SA

- CBG Compagnie Bancaire Geneve

- Caisse d'Epargne Le Cret

- Caisse d'Epargne d'Aubonne

- Caisse d'Epargne de Nyon

- Caisse d'Epargne de Perz

- Caisse d'Epargne de Siviriez

- Caisse d'Epargne de Vuisternenr-devant-Romont

- Caisse d'Epargne de la Ville de Fribourg

- Caisse d'Epargne du District de Cossonay

- Caisse d'Epargne du District de Courtelary

- Caisse d'Epargne du District de Vevey

- Caisse d'Epargne et de Credit Mutuel de Chermignon

- Caisse d'Epargne et de Pervoyance d'Yverdon-les-Bains SA

- Caisse d'Epargne et de Pervoyance de Lausanne

- Canto Consulting

- Cantrade Privatbank AG

- Citibank (Switzerland)

- Citibank N.A.

- Clariden Bank

- Commerzbank (Schweiz)

- Compagnie Bancaire Espirito Santo SA

- Corner Banca SA

- Cosba Private Banking SA

- Coutts & Co. AG

- Credit Suisse

- Credit Suisse First Boston

- Credit Agricole Indosuez (Suisse) SA

- Credit Commercial de France (Suisse)

- Credit Lyonnais (Suisse)

- Credit Mutuel de la Vallee SA

- DC Bank Debosito-Cassa der Stadt Bern

- Dai-Ichi Kangyo Bank

- Deka (Swiss) Privatbank

- Deutsche Bank (Schweiz)

- Deutsche Bank (Suisse)

- Dexia Privatbank

- Direkt Anlage Bank

- Discount Bank and Trust Company

- Dominick Company AG

- Dresdner Bank (Schweiz) AG

- Dreyfus Sohne & Cie

- E. Gutzwiller & Cie. AG

- EB Entlebucher Bank

- EFG Bank European Financial Group

- EFG Private Bank

- Ersparniskasse Breinz

- Ersparnisanstalt Oberuzwil

- Ersparnisanstalt Unterwasser

- Ersparnisanstalt der Stadt St. Gallen

- Ersparniskasseschaft Kuttigen Kuttigen

- Ersparniskasse Affoltern i.E.

- Ersparniskasse Durrenroth

- Ersparniskasse Erlinsbach

- Ersparniskasse Murten

- Ersparniskasse Rueggisberg

- Ersparniskasse Schaffhausen

- Ersparniskasse Speicher

- Ersparniskasse Wyssachen-Eriswil

- Ersparniskasse des Amtsbezirks Interlanke

- Eurasco Bank AG

- F. van Lanschot Bankiers

- FCE Bank

- FIBI Bank

- FTI Banque Fiduciary Trust

- Ferrier Lullin & Cie

- Finansbank (Suisse)

- Finter Bank

- Freie Gemeinschaftsbank BCL

- GE Capital Bank

- GRB Garner Kantonalbank

- Goldman Sachs & Co.

- Gonet & Cie

- Graubunder Kantonalbank

- HSBC Bank Middle East

- HSBC Guyerzeller Bank AG

- HSBC Republic Bank (Suisse) SA

- HYPOSWISS Schweizerische Hypotheken

- Habib Bank AG

- Habibsons Bank Limited

- Handelsfinaz CCF Bank

- Helaba (Schweiz) Landesbank Hessen-Thuringen

- Hentsch Henschoz & Cie

- Hottiner & Cie

- Hypothekarbank Lenzburg

- IBI Bank

- IBZ Bank

- ING Bank N.V.

- ING Baring Private Bank

- IRB Interregiobank

- Instinet (Schweiz) AG

- Investec Bank (Switzerland)

- J.P. Morgan (Suisse) SA

- Jyske Bank

- KGS Sensebank

- Kanz Bank

- Kreditebank

- LT Bank in Liechtenstein

- La Roch & Co. Banquiers

- Landolt & Cie. Banquiers

- Lavoro Bank AG

- Leihkasse Stammheim

- Liechtensteinische Landesbank

- Lienhardt & Partner Privatbank Zurich

- Lloyds TSB Bank plc

- Lombard Odier Darier

- Hentsch & Cie

- Luzerner Kantonalbank

- Luzerner Regiobank AG

- M.M. Warburg Bank

- MIGROSBANK

- Maerki, Baumann & Co.

- Marcurad Cook & Cie. SA

- MediBank

- Merrill Lynch Bank

- Merrill Lynch Capital Markets

- Mirabaud & Cie

- Mitsubishi Tokyo Wealth Management

- Mizuho Bank

- Morgan Guaranty Trust Company of New York

- Morval & Cie. SA

- Mourgue d'Algue & Cie

- National Bank of Kuwait

- Neue Aargauer Bank

- Nidwalder Kantonalbank

- Nomura Bank

- Nordea Bank SA

- Nordfinanz Bank Zurich

- OZ Bankers AG

- Obersimmentalische Volksbank

- Obwalder Kantonalbank

- PBS Privat Bank AG

- PKB Privatbank AG

- Pictet & Cie

- Privatbank Bellerive AG

- Privatbank IHAG Zurich AG

- Privatbank Vermag AG

- Privatbank Von Graffenreied AG

- RBA Zentralbank

- Rabo Robeco Bank

- Rahn & Bodmer

- Redsafe Bank

- Regiobank Solothurn

- Reichmuth & Co.

- Reisebank AG

- Robert Fleming (Switzerland)

- Rothschild Bank AG

- Royal Bank of Canada

- Russische Kommerzial Bank

- RUd, Blass, & Cie

- SB Saanen Bank

- SEB Private Bank

- SG Ruegg Bank

- SIS AGSegaIntersettle

- Sanwa Bank

- Schaffhauser Kantonalbank

- Schmidt Bank

- Schorder &Co. Bank

- Schweizer Verband der Raiffeisenbanken

- Schweizerische Hypotheken

- Schweizerische Nationalbank

- Schweizerische Schiffshyphothenkenbank

- Scwyzer Kantonalbank

- Scobag AG

- Skandia Bank

- Societa Bancaria Ticinese

- Societe Generale

- Solothurner Bank SoBa

- Spar + Leihkasse Frutigen

- Spar + Leihkasse Gurbetal

- Spar und Leihkasse Balgach

- Spar und Leihkasse
  Bucheggberg

- Spar und Leihkasse
  Kaltbrunn

- Spar und Leihkasse
  Kirchberg (SG)

- Spar und Leihkasse Leuk
  und Umgebung

- Spar und Leihkasse
  Madiswil

- Spar und Leihkasse
  Melchnau

- Spar und Leihkasse
  Munsingen

- Spar und Leihkasse Rebstein

- Spar und Leihkasse
  Riggisberg

- Spar und Leihkasse
  Steffisburg

- Spar und Leihkasse
  Sumiswalkd

- Spar und Leihkasse
  Thayngen

- Spar und Liehkasse Wynigen

- Sparcassa 1816

- Spargenossenschft
  Mosnang

- Sparkasse Engleberg

- Sparkasse Horgen

- Sparkasse Kusnacht ZH

- Sparkasse Oberriet

- Sparkasse Oftingen

- Sparkasse Schwyz

- Sparkasse Thalwil

- Sparkasse Trogen

- Sparkasse Wiesendangen

- Sparkasse Zurcher Oberland

- Sparkasse des Sensebezirks

- St. Gallische Creditanstalt

- St. Gallische Kantonalbank
- Swissfirst Bank AG
- Swissquote Bank
- Synthesis Bank
- Tempus Privatbank AG
- The Chase Manhattan Private Bank (Switzerland)
- Thurgauer Kantonalbank
- Tokai Bank (Schweiz) AG
- Trafina Privatbank AG
- Triba Partner Bank
- UBS AG
- UBS Card Center AG
- UEB United European Bank
- UniCredit (Suisse) Bank SA
- Unibank SA
- Union Bancaire Privee

- Untied Bank AG
- United Mizrahi Bank (Schweiz) AG
- Urner Kantonalbank
- VP Bank (Schweiz) AG
- Valiant Bank
- Valiant Privatbank
- Volksbank Bodensee AG
- Vorarlberger Landes und Hypothekenbank AG
- WIR Bank
- Welin & Co. Privatbankiers
- Westdeutsche Landesbank (Schweiz) AG
- ZLB Zurcher Landbank
- Zuger Kantonalbank
- Zurcher Kantonalbank
- Zurich Invest bank AG

Author Biography

Jesse Schmitt is an accomplished freelance writer, published journalist, nationally produced playwright, and author based out of New York City. Jesse has always believed in the power of the individual spirit and is reminded daily that magic is all around us.

Index